15 OF THE GREATEST HOCKEY STORIES EVER FOR KIDS

INSPIRING BIOGRAPHIES, FUN FACTS, THRILLING TRIVIA, QUALITY QUIZZES, AND SHORT STORIES YOU CAN READ IN 5 MINUTES OR LESS. PERFECT FOR CHILDREN AGED 8-12.

TERRIFIC TALES

CONTENTS

ISBN: 978-1-915736-92-5 (Paperback)

ISBN: 978-1-915736-93-2 (Hardcover)

First printing edition 2024. Terrific Tales

admin@terrifictale.com

THIS IS JUST A TASTE OF THE FREE BONUSES INCLUDED

To get all your exciting free bonuses, including extra trivia, fun facts, and quizzes, simply send an email to the address below. As soon as I receive your email, I'll send your bonus material right away!

Email: admin@terrifictale.com

INTRODUCTION

Welcome to *The 15 Greatest Hockey Stories for Kids*! In this book, you're about to dive into some of the most exciting, inspiring, and unforgettable moments in hockey history. From astonishing comebacks to record-breaking achievements, each story will take you to the center of the action, where legends are made and dreams come true. Whether you're a passionate hockey fan or someone who's just discovering the game, these stories will fill you with excitement and awe! Hockey isn't just about scoring goals or winning championships—it's about heart, courage, and teamwork. Every player who steps onto the ice knows that hockey is a game of hard work, resilience, and friendship.

Throughout this book, you'll meet heroes who faced huge challenges but never gave up, teams that came together to achieve the impossible, and individuals who pushed themselves to new heights for the love of the game. These stories are here to remind you that you, too, can achieve great things when you set your mind to it and work together with others.

What makes hockey unique? For one, it's played on ice! Skating at high speeds, handling a puck with a stick, and navigating through opponents requires incredible skill and practice. Every story in this book captures that thrill of gliding across the ice and the challenge of making split-second decisions with the game on the line. Imagine the feeling of charging toward the net, stick in hand, with the crowd roaring around you—it's pure excitement! Hockey players know that there's no substitute for hard work. To make it to the top, they train for hours, learning how to skate faster, handle the puck better, and improve their teamwork. They face setbacks, injuries, and sometimes even doubt, but the love for the game keeps them moving forward. This book will show you stories of players who didn't have it easy but gave it their all. And as you read, you'll realize that the dedication these players have for hockey can be applied to anything in life.

Each chapter in this book tells a story about one of the greatest moments or players in hockey history. These aren't just about the famous games or the biggest championships; they're about the emotions, hard work, and resilience behind every win. You'll learn about heroes like Wayne Gretzky, known as "The Great One," who shattered records and inspired millions with his talent and dedication.

You'll read about "The Miracle on Ice," an event where a group of young, unknown American players came together to defeat a team thought to be unbeatable. These are stories of people who loved hockey so much that they kept going, even when the odds were stacked against them.

HERE'S A TASTE OF WHAT'S WAITING FOR YOU IN THIS BOOK:

- **The Golden Goal**: Imagine the excitement of scoring a game-winning goal for your country. Sidney Crosby did just that in the 2010 Olympics, bringing gold to Canada and creating one of the most unforgettable moments in sports history.
- **The Comeback Kids**: The 1942 Toronto Maple Leafs were down three games in the Stanley Cup Finals. Instead of giving up, they fought back to win the championship, teaching everyone that anything is possible with determination.
- **The Miracle on Ice**: A team of young American college players took on the mighty Soviet team in the 1980 Olympics. What happened next became one of the greatest underdog stories in sports, proving that teamwork and belief can lead to greatness.
- **The Five-Overtime Battle**: In 2000, Keith Primeau of the Philadelphia Flyers scored a goal in the fifth overtime, finally ending one of the longest games in

NHL history. This story shows how hockey players dig deep and find strength even when they're exhausted.

Each story is more than just a recounting of a game. As you read, you'll discover the inspiring life lessons behind each moment: the power of teamwork, the importance of resilience, and the courage to face challenges head-on. These players didn't just win games; they showed the world what it means to push through hard times and believe in yourself.

This book is for you, the hockey fan who wants to learn more about the game's greatest moments. It's for those who love hearing stories of courage and heart and who get excited just thinking about the roar of the crowd and the sound of skates on the ice. As you read, you might find yourself imagining what it would be like to make an incredible play or score a game-winning goal. Let these stories remind you that with hard work and a passion for what you do, you can achieve your own amazing moments, whether in hockey or anything else.

And remember, these stories aren't just about winning; they're about the journey, the challenges, and the lessons learned along the way. You'll see how players handle both triumph and failure, and you'll realize that everyone, even the greatest hockey legends, faces challenges. The difference is that they kept going, stayed focused, and believed in themselves.

So, are you ready to dive into the world of hockey legends and amazing achievements? As you flip through the pages, you'll find yourself transported to the ice, right there with the players as they make history. You'll learn about the moments that made hockey the incredible sport it is today and meet heroes who showed us that anything is possible with determination and heart.

This book is your ticket to discovering the magic of hockey's greatest stories. Whether you're a new fan or a lifelong hockey enthusiast, these tales will keep you captivated, inspired, and eager to learn more about this amazing sport. So lace up your skates, grab your stick, and turn the page—there's a whole world of hockey waiting for you to explore!

CHAPTER 1
THE MIRACLE ON ICE

IMAGINE PLAYING THE MOST IMPORTANT GAME OF YOUR LIFE against a team that seems unstoppable. That's exactly what happened to a group of young American hockey players in 1980. The U.S. men's Olympic hockey team wasn't expected to win a medal, let alone defeat the greatest team in the world —the Soviet Union. No one thought they had a chance. But on February 22, 1980, these underdogs shocked the world in a game that would go down in history as "The Miracle on Ice."

This isn't just a story about hockey; it's about believing in yourself, working as a team, and proving that nothing is impossible when you give it your all.

MIKE ERUZIONE
"RIZZO"
TEAM CAPTAIN
USA

The 1980 Winter Olympics were held in a small town called Lake Placid in New York. Countries from all over the world sent their best athletes to compete in sports like skiing, figure skating, and, of course, hockey. Hockey was one of the most exciting events, and in the 1970s and 1980s, the Soviet Union was by far the best hockey team in the world. They had won the gold medal in four straight Olympics and had some of the greatest players in history. These players were professionals who had trained together for years. They played hockey full-time, and they were fast, tough, and nearly unbeatable.

In contrast, the U.S. Olympic team was made up of college players. Most of them were in their early twenties, and they weren't professionals. Many of these players came from places like Minnesota, Massachusetts, and Michigan, where hockey was popular, but none of them were superstars. In fact, most people had never even heard of them before the Olympics. The team's coach, Herb Brooks, knew that they weren't as skilled as the Soviets, but he believed something else could give them a chance: teamwork and hard work.

Herb Brooks was a tough coach who didn't care about being liked. He wanted to push his team to its limits. He believed that if they worked harder than anyone else, and played together as one, they might be able to surprise the world. But the road to the Olympics wasn't easy.

The U.S. team faced an almost impossible challenge. When the Olympics began, no one really expected much from them.

Just a few weeks before the tournament, they played an exhibition game against the Soviet Union at Madison Square Garden in New York. The result? A humiliating 10-3 loss. The Soviets completely dominated them, making it look like the Americans didn't even belong on the same ice.

But Herb Brooks wasn't discouraged. He continued to push his players, making practices as tough as possible. One of his most famous drills was something the players called "Herbies," where they had to skate up and down the ice over and over until they were completely exhausted. Brooks wasn't just trying to improve their skating; he was teaching them mental toughness. He wanted his players to be able to handle anything, even if it seemed impossible. As the Olympic tournament started, something amazing happened. The U.S. team began to play better than anyone expected. In their first game, they managed a 2-2 tie against Sweden, which was a strong team. After that, they shocked the world by beating Czechoslovakia, one of the top teams in the world, by a score of 7-3. Suddenly, people started paying attention. Maybe this team of young, unknown players was better than everyone thought.

But no one really believed they could beat the Soviet Union, who had continued to dominate their opponents. The U.S. team knew that if they wanted to win a medal, they would have to face the Soviets in the semifinals. It seemed like an impossible task.

The Soviet players were bigger, stronger, faster, and more experienced. But there was one thing the U.S. team had that the Soviets didn't: hope.

The game between the United States and the Soviet Union took place on February 22, 1980. It was the semifinals, and the winner would advance to the gold medal game. Coach Herb Brooks gave a powerful speech before the game. He told his players that this was their moment. "You were born to be a player. You were meant to be here. This moment is yours," he said. The players believed in him, and they believed in each other.

The game started, and as expected, the Soviets came out strong. They scored the first goal, and it looked like the U.S. team was in trouble. But the Americans didn't give up. They fought hard and tied the game 1-1. The Soviets quickly regained the lead, making it 2-1, but just before the first period ended, U.S. player Mark Johnson scored a goal with only one second left on the clock. The game was tied again at 2-2, and suddenly, the impossible seemed possible.

In the second period, the Soviets took control again, making it 3-2, but the U.S. players didn't lose hope. Jim Craig, the U.S. goaltender, made save after save, keeping the game close. The Soviet players were faster and stronger, but the U.S. team had heart and determination.

The third period was where history was made. With just over ten minutes left in the game, Mark Johnson tied the game at 3-3. The crowd was on its feet, cheering louder than ever. Then, with 10 minutes left on the clock, U.S. team captain Mike Eruzione took a shot that would change history. He fired the puck past the Soviet goalie, and the U.S. took the lead for the first time in the game—4-3!

The final ten minutes were some of the most intense moments in hockey history. The Soviets were desperate to tie the game, and they threw everything they had at the U.S. defense. But Jim Craig stood tall in goal, making save after save. Every second felt like an eternity as the U.S. team tried to hold onto their lead. The clock slowly ticked down, and with just a few seconds left, the crowd could hardly contain its excitement.

As the final buzzer rang, the U.S. team had done the impossible. They had defeated the mighty Soviet Union! The players threw their gloves and sticks in the air, celebrating what would become known as The Miracle on Ice. The crowd was cheering, and people across the country were glued to their televisions, watching in disbelief. It was one of the greatest upsets in sports history.

The Miracle on Ice wasn't just about winning a hockey game. It was about proving that anything is possible when you work hard, believe in yourself, and play as a team. The U.S. team went on to win the gold medal, defeating Finland in the final.

But it was the victory over the Soviets that everyone would remember. For the players, it was a dream come true. They weren't the biggest, fastest, or most talented team, but they had heart and determination. Coach Herb Brooks had pushed them to their limits, and they had proven that they could achieve something no one thought was possible. The Miracle on Ice became a symbol of hope, not just for hockey fans, but for the entire country. It showed that underdogs could achieve greatness.

The story of the 1980 U.S. Olympic hockey team is a reminder that no matter how tough things may seem, you should never give up. Even when the odds are against you, anything is possible if you work hard, believe in yourself, and support your teammates. The Miracle on Ice wasn't just a victory for the U.S. team; it was a victory for anyone who has ever faced a challenge and refused to back down. So the next time you're facing something that feels impossible, remember the story of the Miracle on Ice—and believe in your own ability to create miracles. (Roos & Roos, 2024).

> "We weren't afraid of anybody. We respected them, but we felt confident we could play with anyone."
>
> MARK JOHNSON

CAREER HIGHLIGHTS

Mike Eruzione (Captain)

• Decided to retire from hockey after the 1980 Olympics, choosing not to play professionally.

• Became a broadcaster and motivational speaker, sharing the story of the Miracle on Ice with audiences worldwide.

Jim Craig (Goaltender)

• Went on to play in the NHL with the Atlanta Flames, Boston Bruins, and Minnesota North Stars.

Mark Johnson (Forward)

• Had a successful NHL career with teams like the Pittsburgh Penguins and New Jersey Devils.

Jack O'Callahan (Defenseman)

• Played in the NHL for the Chicago Blackhawks and New Jersey Devils.

Ken Morrow (Defenseman)

• Immediately joined the NHL's New York Islanders after the Olympics, winning four consecutive Stanley Cups from 1980 to 1983.

Dave Christian (Forward)

• Had a successful NHL career with teams including the Winnipeg Jets, Washington Capitals, and Boston Bruins.

• Scored over 300 goals in the NHL and became known for his consistent performance and work ethic.

Neal Broten (Forward)

• Played in the NHL for the Minnesota North Stars, Dallas Stars, and New Jersey Devils.

• Became the first American player to score over 100 points in an NHL season and won a Stanley Cup with the Devils in 1995.

Mike Ramsey (Defenseman)

• Went on to have a long NHL career, primarily with the Buffalo Sabres and later with the Pittsburgh Penguins and Detroit Red Wings.

Rob McClanahan (Forward)

•Played in the NHL for the Buffalo Sabres, Hartford Whalers, and New York Rangers.

CHAPTER 2
THE FLYING GOAL

It was Game 4 of the Stanley Cup Finals in 1970. The Boston Bruins were on the verge of winning their first championship in 29 years. With the game tied in overtime, every player on the ice knew that one goal could change everything. The puck glided across the ice toward the Bruins' best player—Bobby Orr. He skated forward with lightning speed, dodging defenders as if they weren't even there. And then it happened. In one incredible moment, Bobby Orr scored the game-winning goal, launching himself into the air as if he could fly. The crowd went wild as Orr soared through the air, arms stretched out, making it one of the most famous goals in hockey history. But Bobby Orr's journey to becoming a legend wasn't always easy.

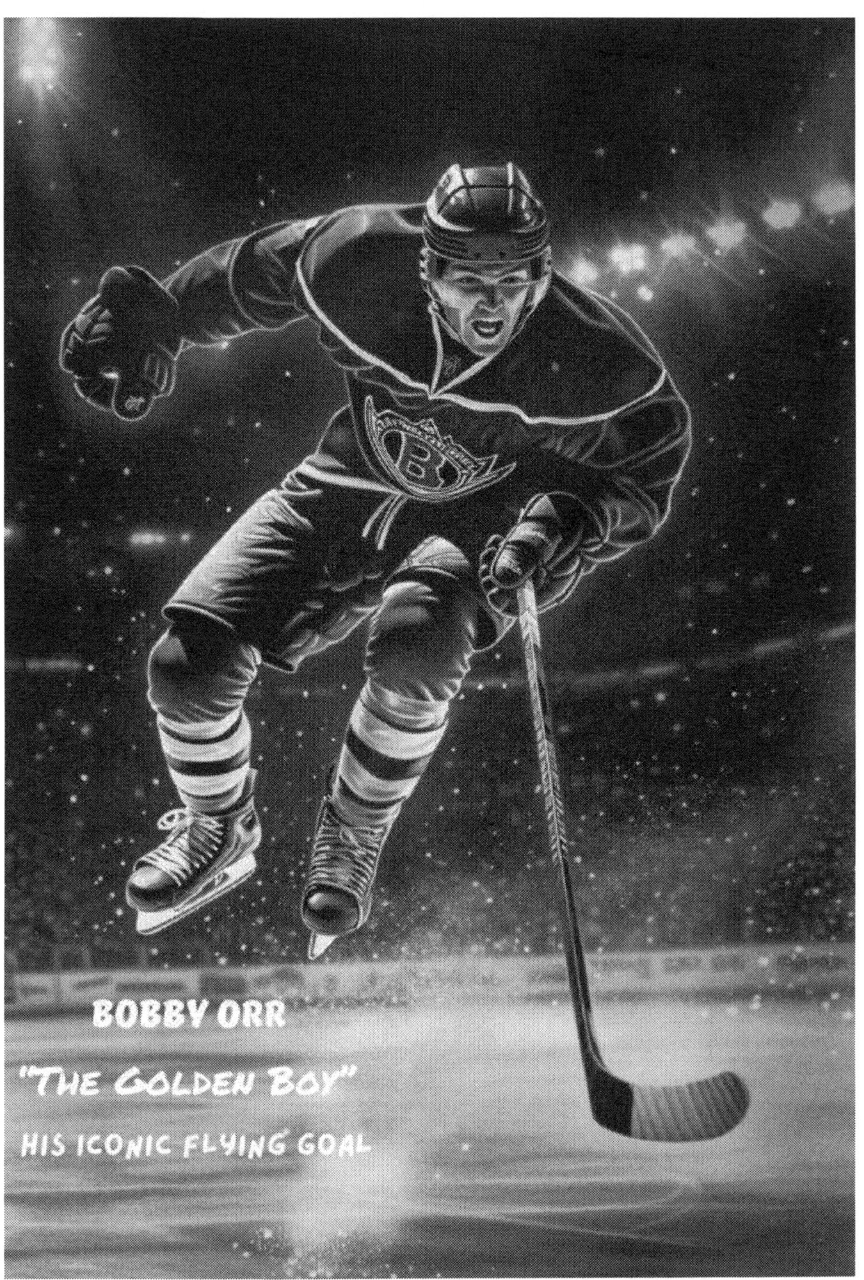
BOBBY ORR
"THE GOLDEN BOY"
HIS ICONIC FLYING GOAL

Bobby Orr grew up in the small town of Parry Sound, Ontario, Canada. From a young age, everyone could tell that Bobby was special when it came to hockey. He was fast, strong, and had an incredible ability to see the game in ways that others couldn't. Most defensemen at the time played cautiously, staying back near their goal to protect it from opposing players. But Bobby was different. He was a defenseman who attacked, using his speed to move the puck up the ice and create scoring chances. This style of play would change hockey forever.

Even though he had natural talent, Bobby worked harder than anyone else. He spent countless hours practicing his skating and stickhandling on frozen ponds during the long Canadian winters. But it wasn't just his skill that set him apart; it was his determination and love for the game. Bobby's dream was to one day play in the National Hockey League (NHL) and help his team win the Stanley Cup.

By the time he was 14, Bobby was already playing against older, stronger players in junior hockey leagues, where he quickly became known as one of the best young players in Canada. Scouts from the NHL took notice, and soon, the Boston Bruins signed him to play for their team. But even as he entered the NHL, Bobby faced challenges that tested his strength and willpower.

When Bobby Orr joined the Boston Bruins in 1966, the team was far from being the best in the league. In fact, they were one of the worst teams, and they hadn't won a Stanley Cup since 1941. The pressure was on Bobby to help turn the team around. As a rookie, he made an immediate impact, but the team still struggled to win games. Bobby knew that his dream of winning the Stanley Cup was far from becoming a reality.

On top of the team's struggles, Bobby had to deal with personal challenges. By the time he was 20 years old, Bobby's knees were starting to give him trouble. Hockey is a tough, physical sport, and the constant hits and intense skating had taken a toll on his body. Bobby had to undergo several surgeries on his knees, and the pain was constant. Some people wondered if he could continue playing at such a high level. But Bobby Orr wasn't someone who gave up easily. He worked even harder to stay in shape and keep his legs strong. He knew that if he could push through the pain, he could help lead his team to victory. Even though the injuries were tough, Bobby's love for the game and his determination to win the Stanley Cup kept him going.

By the time the 1969-1970 season rolled around, Bobby and the Bruins were finally ready to compete for the championship. With Bobby leading the charge, the Bruins dominated the league, finishing with one of the best records in hockey. But the real test was yet to come—the Stanley Cup playoffs. The Bruins breezed through the first two rounds, and before long, they found themselves in the Stanley Cup Finals against the St. Louis Blues. This was Bobby's chance to make his dream come true, but it wouldn't be easy.

The Stanley Cup Finals were intense, and the Blues fought hard to keep up with the Bruins. But by Game 4, the Bruins had taken a commanding 3-0 series lead, and one more win would give them the championship. The game was close, with both teams battling for every inch of the ice. By the time the third period ended, the score was tied 3-3, and the game went into overtime.

As Bobby Orr laced up his skates for overtime, he knew that this was his moment. He had worked his entire life for a chance like this—to win the Stanley Cup for his team and his city. The entire game came down to just one goal. He remembered everything he had fought through—his injuries, the team's struggles, and all the hard work that had brought him to this point. Bobby was ready. Coach Harry Sinden reminded the team to stay focused, and the Bruins took to the ice determined to end the game. Every player was exhausted, but Bobby's heart was full of fire. He knew this was the chance to make history.

Just 40 seconds into overtime, Bobby saw his chance. Teammate Derek Sanderson had the puck behind the Blues' net, and Bobby skated forward, ready for the pass. Sanderson sent the puck sliding toward the front of the goal, and Bobby raced toward it. As soon as it reached his stick, Bobby took the shot.

The puck flew toward the net, and before anyone had time to react, it sailed past Blues goaltender Glenn Hall and into the goal.

The crowd erupted in cheers as Bobby Orr leaped into the air in celebration, but just as he jumped, Blues defenseman Noel Picard tripped him, causing Bobby to go flying through the air. In that incredible moment, Bobby Orr soared with his arms stretched out, perfectly capturing the excitement and joy of winning the Stanley Cup. It was a goal that would be remembered forever, and the image of Bobby Orr flying through the air became one of the most iconic photos in sports history.

The Boston Bruins had won the Stanley Cup! Bobby Orr had not only scored the winning goal, but he had done it in a way that people would talk about for generations. The Bruins rushed onto the ice to celebrate with Bobby, and the fans in Boston celebrated long into the night. After 29 years, the Stanley Cup was finally back in Boston.

For Bobby Orr, the flying goal was more than just a game-winning shot—it was the result of years of hard work, determination, and overcoming adversity. He had faced injuries, doubters, and the pressure of leading a struggling team. But through it all, Bobby never gave up on his dream of winning the Stanley Cup. Bobby's flying goal taught him that success doesn't come easy. It takes dedication, perseverance, and sometimes a little bit of pain.

His love for hockey pushed him to work harder than anyone else, even when things got tough. And in the end, all that hard work paid off. Bobby Orr would go on to have a Hall of Fame career, becoming one of the greatest hockey players of all time. But it was the lessons he learned from his challenges that shaped him as both a player and a person. His story shows that no matter how difficult the journey may seem, anything is possible if you believe in yourself and work hard.

Bobby Orr's flying goal is more than just a famous moment in sports history. It's a reminder that no matter how tough things get, you can achieve your dreams if you're willing to put in the work. Bobby didn't let injuries or obstacles stop him from becoming a champion, and you shouldn't let anything stand in the way of your goals.

Remember, whether you're playing sports, studying for a test, or chasing any dream, hard work and belief in yourself can take you farther than you ever imagined. Like Bobby Orr, you can make history. All you have to do is keep pushing, never give up, and believe in your ability to soar. (Johnson, 2024).

> The biggest thing I learned from hockey is that you have to rely on your team and they have to rely on you.
>
> BOBBY ORR

CAREER HIGHLIGHTS

- **Young Phenom**: Joined the Oshawa Generals at 14, then signed with the Boston Bruins at 18, entering the NHL with immense promise.
- **NHL Rookie of the Year**: Won the Calder Memorial Trophy as the league's best rookie in the 1966-67 season.
- **First Defenseman to Score 100 Points**: Became the first defenseman in NHL history to score over 100 points in a season, achieving this milestone six times.
- **Two-Time Stanley Cup Champion**: Won Stanley Cups with the Boston Bruins in 1970 and 1972, with his famous "Flying Goal" in the 1970 Finals.
- **Norris Trophy Dominance**: Claimed the Norris Trophy as the NHL's best defenseman for eight consecutive years (1968-1975), a record that still stands.
- **Two-Time Hart Trophy Winner**: Earned the Hart Trophy as the NHL's Most Valuable Player in 1970 and 1971.
- **Conn Smythe Trophy and Scoring Records**: Led the league in points and won the Conn Smythe Trophy as playoff MVP twice, in 1970 and 1972.
- **Hall of Fame Induction**: Inducted into the Hockey Hall of Fame in 1979, with the traditional waiting period waived.

CHAPTER 3

THE GREAT ONE HITS 802

IT WAS A MOMENT THE ENTIRE HOCKEY WORLD HAD BEEN waiting for. On March 23, 1994, Wayne Gretzky, known as "The Great One," stood just one goal away from breaking the most prestigious record in hockey: the all-time goal-scoring record of 801 goals held by his idol, Gordie Howe. As the puck moved across the ice, fans in the arena held their breath. Everyone knew that Gretzky had a chance to do something special. With his Los Angeles Kings teammates racing down the ice, Gretzky skated into position. And then, with a flick of his wrist, he made history. His 802nd goal wasn't just another point—it was the moment Wayne Gretzky officially became the greatest goal scorer in NHL history. But how did he get here?

WAYNE GRETZKY
"THE GREAT ONE"
SCORES GOAL NUMBER 802

Wayne Gretzky was born in a small town in Canada called Brantford, Ontario. Even as a little boy, it was clear that Wayne was something special. His father, Walter Gretzky, built an ice rink in their backyard, and Wayne spent hours practicing his skating and shooting every day. While most kids were out playing with their friends, Wayne was studying the game, trying to master the skills he would one day use in the NHL. By the time he was ten years old, Wayne was already scoring over 300 goals in a single season for his youth hockey team! People around him started calling him "The Great One" because he was better than anyone they had ever seen.

As Wayne grew older, he continued to break records and amaze everyone who watched him play. He joined the Edmonton Oilers when he was 18 years old and helped them win four Stanley Cup championships. Wayne wasn't the biggest or fastest player on the ice, but he had an incredible ability to see plays developing before anyone else did. His vision, hockey sense, and creativity made him the most dominant player in the league. He set record after record, and by the time he was 33 years old, Wayne had already scored more goals and points than most players ever dream of.

But one record still stood in his way: Gordie Howe's all-time goal record of 801. Gordie Howe, also known as "Mr. Hockey," was a legend. He played professional hockey for over 30 years, and his 801 goals were considered untouchable.

No one believed anyone could break that record—until Wayne came along. Gretzky knew that surpassing Gordie Howe's record would be the ultimate achievement in his career. But reaching that point was no easy task. By the time the 1993-94 season rolled around, Wayne was in the twilight of his career, playing for the Los Angeles Kings. His time in the NHL had been full of success, but it also came with challenges. In 1988, he was traded from the Edmonton Oilers to the Kings in a move that shocked the entire hockey world. Edmonton was where Wayne had won championships and set records, and moving to Los Angeles was a tough adjustment. But like always, Gretzky didn't let adversity stop him.

He led the Kings to the Stanley Cup Finals in 1993 and continued to play at an elite level, even as he got older. But there was another challenge Wayne had to face—his body. After years of playing the game at such a high level, injuries began to take their toll. He wasn't the young, invincible player he once was, and he had to work harder than ever to keep up with the fast pace of the game. His back was constantly sore, and the long NHL season was exhausting. Despite this, Wayne never stopped believing in himself. He knew that if he kept playing his game, he would have a chance to break Howe's record. As the 1993-94 season progressed, Wayne's goal total climbed closer and closer to 801. With each game, the anticipation grew. The media followed his every move, fans packed arenas to watch history unfold, and his teammates supported him every step of the way.

Finally, after scoring his 801st goal, Wayne was tied with Gordie Howe. All he needed was one more goal to make history. But that last goal wouldn't come easy. For a few games, Wayne struggled to find the back of the net. He had several chances to score but was either stopped by the goalie or the puck just missed the net. The pressure began to build. Would Wayne finally break the record, or would the pressure be too much to handle?

Everything changed on March 23, 1994. The Los Angeles Kings were playing against the Vancouver Canucks at the Great Western Forum in Los Angeles. Wayne knew that the entire hockey world was watching him, waiting for that moment when he would finally surpass Gordie Howe's legendary record. The game was intense, with both teams battling for control of the puck. But Wayne kept his cool. He had been in high-pressure situations before and knew that if he played his game, the goal would come. In the second period, with the score tied, Gretzky saw an opportunity. His teammate, Marty McSorley, passed the puck to him, and Wayne quickly skated toward the net. Time seemed to slow down as Wayne took the shot.

The puck sailed past the goalie and into the net. The crowd erupted in cheers, and Wayne raised his arms in celebration. He had done it—802 goals, more than any player in the history of the NHL.

The arena buzzed with excitement as Gretzky's teammates surrounded him, congratulating him on his achievement. But for Wayne, it wasn't just about the goal; it was about everything that led him to that moment—his hard work, dedication, and love for the game. As the celebration continued, the moment finally began to sink in. Wayne Gretzky had achieved the impossible. Gordie Howe's record, which had stood for decades, was now in the hands of "The Great One." Wayne stood at center ice, looking out at the crowd, who were all on their feet, cheering and clapping for him. The love and admiration from the fans were overwhelming.

As Wayne skated around the ice, he knew this wasn't just a victory for himself—it was a victory for everyone who had supported him throughout his career. His family, his coaches, his teammates, and, of course, the fans who had believed in him every step of the way. Breaking the all-time goal-scoring record was more than just a personal achievement; it was a moment that cemented Wayne Gretzky's legacy as the greatest hockey player of all time.

After the game, Wayne spoke to the crowd, thanking them for their support. "It's an honor to be mentioned in the same breath as Gordie Howe," he said. But in that moment, everyone knew that Wayne Gretzky had become the new face of hockey—a player who not only broke records but also inspired generations of kids to believe that anything was possible.

Wayne's 802nd goal wasn't just a record-breaking moment—it was the culmination of years of hard work, perseverance, and a passion for the game. Wayne didn't become "The Great One" overnight. It took countless hours of practice, determination, and a belief that he could be the best. Throughout his career, Wayne faced challenges, from injuries to the pressure of being the best player in the world. But he never let those challenges stop him from achieving greatness. The lesson here is simple: if you work hard and believe in yourself, you can achieve your dreams, just like Wayne did. Breaking Gordie Howe's record was an incredible accomplishment, but it wouldn't have happened without Wayne's dedication to the game he loved.

Wayne Gretzky's 802nd goal is a reminder that no dream is too big if you're willing to work for it. Whether you're playing hockey, studying for school, or chasing any other goal, remember that the journey is just as important as the destination. Wayne didn't give up when things got tough, and neither should you. So the next time you face a challenge, think of Gretzky and his 802 goals, and remember that with hard work, anything is possible. You can break your own records—just like "The Great One." (Stubbs, 2024).

You miss 100% of the shots you don't take.

WAYNE GRETZKY

CAREER HIGHLIGHTS

- **Junior Hockey Phenom**: Dominated junior hockey with the Sault Ste. Marie Greyhounds, scoring 182 points in his only season and wearing his iconic number 99 for the first time.
- **NHL Debut and Immediate Impact**: Joined the NHL with the Edmonton Oilers in 1979, quickly proving his skill with a record-breaking 137-point season as a rookie.
- **First NHL Scoring Title**: Won his first Art Ross Trophy as the league's leading scorer in 1981, marking the beginning of a record ten scoring titles.
- **Single-Season Points Record**: Set an NHL record with 215 points in a single season (1985-86), a record that remains unbroken.
- **Stanley Cup Championships**: Led the Edmonton Oilers to four Stanley Cup titles (1984, 1985, 1987, 1988), solidifying his place as one of the all-time greats.
- **Breaking Gordie Howe's Record**: Surpassed Gordie Howe's record of 1,850 career points in 1989, setting a new benchmark for career scoring.
- **All-Time Goals Record**: Set the all-time NHL record for career goals with his 802nd goal in 1994, eventually finishing with 894 goals.

- **Career Assist and Points Leader**: Retired with 1,963 assists and 2,857 points, both of which are all-time records that remain unchallenged.
- **Nine Hart Trophies**: Awarded the Hart Trophy as the NHL's Most Valuable Player a record nine times, underscoring his impact on the game.
- **Hockey Hall of Fame Induction**: Inducted into the Hockey Hall of Fame in 1999, with the waiting period waived in recognition of his achievements.

CHAPTER 4
THE GOLDEN GOAL

ALRIGHT, BEFORE WE DIVE INTO THIS STORY, I NEED TO ISSUE a sincere apology to all the U.S. hockey fans reading this. We're about to revisit a certain moment from the 2010 Winter Olympics that might still sting. Yes, we're talking about the Golden Goal—the one that Sidney Crosby scored in overtime to give Team Canada the gold medal in Vancouver.

SIDNEY CROSBY
"THE NEXT ONE"
THE GOLDEN GOAL

The whole world held its breath as Sidney Crosby raced down the ice. It was the gold medal game of the 2010 Winter Olympics in Vancouver, and Team Canada was tied 2-2 with Team USA. Overtime was underway, and the next goal would decide who took home the gold. The pressure was on—Sidney, one of the best players in the world, had the puck on his stick. Time seemed to slow down as he made his move. He fired a quick shot, and the puck slipped past the American goalie. *GOAL!* The crowd erupted in joy, and Sidney Crosby had just scored the most important goal of his career—the Golden Goal. Canada had won Olympic gold in hockey, and Crosby was the hero. But what led to this unforgettable moment?

Sidney was born in Cole Harbour, Nova Scotia, a small Canadian town where hockey was more than just a sport—it was a way of life. From the time he could walk, Sidney was obsessed with hockey. His father, Troy Crosby, had played hockey at a high level, and he passed his love for the game down to Sidney. By the time he was just two years old, he was already skating on his family's backyard rink. He practiced endlessly, shooting pucks in the basement and skating for hours.

Sidney's talent was obvious to everyone who saw him play. By the time he was seven years old, he was scoring goals by the dozens in his youth hockey league. People started calling him a hockey prodigy, and it wasn't long before Sidney was recognized as one of the best young players in Canada. His hard work and dedication to the sport were unmatched, and he dreamed of one day playing in the NHL.

As Sidney grew older, his skills continued to develop. He was drafted by the Pittsburgh Penguins in 2005 and made an immediate impact, becoming the youngest captain in NHL history to win the Stanley Cup in 2009. But Sidney wasn't just playing for himself—he had the hopes of an entire country resting on his shoulders. In 2010, Sidney would lead Team Canada into the Winter Olympics, held in Vancouver, with the goal of bringing home the gold medal. Canada had a rich history in hockey and was the favorite to win gold, but there was a lot of pressure on him. Everyone expected him to perform, and the entire nation was counting on him. Could he rise to the occasion?

The 2010 Winter Olympics were filled with challenges for Sidney and Team Canada. Hockey is the heart and soul of Canadian sports, and winning the gold medal on home soil meant everything to the country. But the competition was fierce. Teams like Russia, Sweden, and especially Team USA were all serious contenders. The games were intense, and every team wanted to beat Canada, especially in front of a home crowd. As the tournament progressed, Team Canada showed flashes of brilliance but also struggled at times. They lost a heartbreaker to the United States in the group stage, putting them in a tough position moving forward.

Many people started to wonder if Canada had what it took to win the gold. Sidney felt the pressure mounting. As Canada's best player, he knew that the entire country was counting on him to deliver. In the knockout stages, Canada began to find their rhythm. They defeated Russia in a commanding win and then beat Slovakia in the semifinals to set up a gold medal showdown with their biggest rivals, Team USA. The stage was set for an epic final.

The gold medal game was played in front of a raucous home crowd in Vancouver, with millions of Canadians watching at home. The game itself was tense from the start. Team USA was determined to spoil Canada's party, and both teams fought hard. Jonathan Toews scored for Canada in the first period, and Corey Perry added another goal in the second. But Team USA never gave up. With just seconds left in the game, U.S. forward Zach Parise scored to tie the game at 2-2, sending it to overtime. Suddenly, the game that was almost won had become a nerve-wracking overtime battle. The next goal would decide everything. For Sidney and Team Canada, the pressure couldn't have been greater.

Overtime in the Olympic gold medal game is a moment few players ever get to experience. The entire arena was on edge, knowing that one mistake or one brilliant play could make all the difference. For Sidney, this was the moment he had dreamed of his whole life. He knew that this was his chance to do something special for his team and his country.

As the overtime period began, both teams came out strong. Every pass, every shot, every defensive play was crucial. The tension was unbearable, but Crosby remained calm. He had been in big moments before, but nothing like this. Canada needed a hero, and Sidney was ready.

The turning point came just a few minutes into overtime. Sidney had been relatively quiet during the game, but he was always lurking, waiting for his opportunity. Suddenly, the puck found its way to him. He raced down the ice with his teammate Jarome Iginla nearby. Sidney shouted, "Iggy!" to Iginla, calling for the pass. Iginla heard him and quickly slid the puck toward him. This was it. Sidney took the puck on his stick, moved swiftly past the defenders, and fired a quick shot toward the goal. The puck slipped past Ryan Miller, the U.S. goalie, and into the net. GOAL!

The moment the puck crossed the goal line, the entire arena erupted in deafening cheers. Sidney had just scored the Golden Goal, securing the gold medal for Team Canada! Players threw their gloves and sticks into the air, rushing toward Crosby in celebration. The crowd was going wild, and Canada had finally done it—they had won Olympic gold on home soil.

For Sidney, it was the moment of a lifetime. As he skated toward his teammates, arms raised in triumph, the weight of the pressure he had been carrying was lifted. He had delivered in the biggest moment of his career.

The "Golden Goal" instantly became a legendary moment, not just in Canadian hockey, but in sports history. The celebration went on for hours. Fans across Canada celebrated in the streets, waving flags and cheering as loud as they could. Sidney had become a national hero. His goal wasn't just a win for the team—it was a win for the entire country. Canada had reclaimed its place at the top of the hockey world, and Sidney Crosby's name would forever be remembered as the player who delivered one of the greatest moments in Olympic history.

Sidney's Golden Goal wasn't just about winning a gold medal. It was a story of perseverance, teamwork, and handling pressure in the most intense moment. He had faced challenges throughout the tournament, including the tough loss to Team USA in the group stage. But he never let the pressure break him. Instead, he used it to fuel his determination to win.

His moment of glory teaches us that even in the most difficult situations, we can rise to the occasion if we stay focused and believe in ourselves. Sidney knew that he had the support of his teammates and the entire nation, and that gave him the strength to deliver when it mattered most.

His goal was a result of years of hard work, practice, and dedication to the sport he loved. Sidney's Golden Goal is a reminder that even in the toughest moments, you have the power to achieve greatness. Whether you're playing hockey, studying for a test, or facing any kind of challenge, remember that hard work and belief in yourself can lead to amazing things. Sidney didn't give up when the pressure was on, and neither should you. So, the next time you're faced with a big moment, know that you, too, can shine when it matters most.

("Remembering Sidney Crosby's Golden Goal," 2017).

I just love to play the game. I just love competing and challenging myself every day.

SIDNEY CROSBY

CAREER HIGHLIGHTS

- **Junior Hockey Standout**: Dominated with the Rimouski Océanic in the Quebec Major Junior Hockey League (QMJHL), earning the nickname "The Next One" for his extraordinary skill.
- **First Overall NHL Draft Pick**: Drafted first overall by the Pittsburgh Penguins in 2005, immediately sparking hope for the franchise.
- **Youngest NHL Captain to Win the Stanley Cup**: Led the Pittsburgh Penguins to a Stanley Cup victory in 2009 at the age of 21, becoming the youngest captain to achieve this feat.
- **Two-Time Olympic Gold Medalist**: Won Olympic gold with Team Canada in 2010 and 2014, including

scoring the legendary "Golden Goal" in overtime against the USA in the 2010 Vancouver Olympics.

- **Back-to-Back Stanley Cups and Conn Smythe Trophies**: Led the Penguins to consecutive Stanley Cup championships in 2016 and 2017, winning the Conn Smythe Trophy as the playoff MVP both times.
- **Multiple Art Ross, Hart, and Ted Lindsay Trophies**: Awarded the Art Ross Trophy (scoring leader), Hart Trophy (MVP), and Ted Lindsay Award (most outstanding player, voted by peers) multiple times throughout his career.
- **1,000 Career Points Milestone**: Reached 1,000 career points in 2017, becoming one of the youngest players in NHL history to do so.
- **Mark Messier Leadership Award**: Honored in 2010 with the Mark Messier Leadership Award, recognizing his dedication, sportsmanship, and leadership on and off the ice.

CHAPTER 5
THE 10 POINT NIGHT

IT WAS A COLD NIGHT ON FEBRUARY 7, 1976, AND THE Toronto Maple Leafs were about to play the Boston Bruins at Maple Leaf Gardens. Nobody could have predicted that this ordinary game would turn into one of the most historic moments in hockey history. By the end of the night, the name Darryl Sittler would be etched in the record books forever. Sittler, the Leafs' captain, put on a performance unlike anything anyone had ever seen. He didn't just score a goal or two—he racked up 10 points in a single game, a feat that has never been matched. But how did he do it? What led to the most legendary game of Darryl Sittler's career?

DARRYL SITTLER
"SITTS"
10-POINT NIGHT

***Note** - A hockey point is a way to keep track of a player's or team's contributions during a game. It's a simple system that combines goals and assists.*

Darryl Sittler grew up in a small town in St. Jacobs, Ontario, where hockey was the heartbeat of every winter. From a young age, Darryl fell in love with the sport. His parents built him an ice rink in the backyard, where he spent countless hours practicing his shots, skating, and dreaming of one day playing in the National Hockey League (NHL). He was a natural on the ice, with a quick shot and smooth skating ability that set him apart from his peers.

As a teenager, Sittler joined junior hockey leagues and continued to impress everyone who saw him play. His hard work and dedication paid off when he was drafted by the Toronto Maple Leafs in 1970. Sittler quickly became one of the team's top players, and by 1975, he was named the team's captain. The Leafs were one of the most storied franchises in the NHL, but they hadn't won a Stanley Cup since 1967. The pressure was on for Sittler to lead his team to victory.

Sittler wasn't the biggest or the flashiest player in the league, but he had an incredible work ethic and was known for his leadership on and off the ice. He believed in teamwork and always put his team first. But on February 7, 1976, Sittler was about to show the world that he could be a superstar too.

The 1975-76 season had been up and down for the Toronto Maple Leafs. While they had some strong players, they struggled with consistency, and the pressure was always on for them to perform better. Darryl Sittler, as the captain, felt the weight of responsibility. He knew the team was looking to him to lead them through tough times, and he took that role seriously.

Leading up to the game against the Boston Bruins, Sittler had been solid but not spectacular. He knew he needed to push himself to another level if he wanted to help the Leafs make a deep playoff run that year. The Bruins were one of the league's toughest teams, known for their physical play and skillful lineup, including legendary players like Bobby Orr.

Toronto fans were hungry for a win, and the atmosphere in Maple Leaf Gardens was electric, as it always was when the Bruins came to town. The Leafs knew they had to bring their best effort to compete with a team as strong as Boston. But nobody could have predicted what was about to happen next—especially Darryl Sittler.

From the very start of the game, something felt different. Sittler was flying up and down the ice, setting up plays and looking for opportunities. Early in the first period, he scored a goal, giving the Leafs an early lead. The crowd erupted, cheering for their captain. But Sittler wasn't done. Moments later, he assisted on another goal, then another.

By the end of the first period, Sittler already had four points —a huge night by anyone's standards. As the second period began, Sittler kept up the pressure. His passes were crisp, his skating was smooth, and he seemed to be involved in every play. He scored again, and then again. He assisted on another goal, and before long, he had eight points. The crowd could hardly believe what they were seeing. With the game firmly in hand for the Maple Leafs, the question wasn't whether they would win, but just how many points Darryl Sittler could collect. His teammates fed him the puck, knowing something special was happening. Sittler's confidence grew with each shift, and every time he touched the puck, it felt like magic.

As the third period began, Sittler knew he was close to breaking the NHL record for the most points in a single game. But he didn't focus on the record—he just kept playing his game, determined to help his team finish strong. The third period was when Darryl Sittler cemented his place in hockey history. He already had eight points, but the record was within reach. With his teammates rallying behind him, Sittler continued to dominate. He scored another goal to make it nine points, tying the record for most points in a game, set by Maurice "Rocket" Richard in 1944.

But Sittler wasn't done. With just a few minutes left in the game, he saw another opportunity. He charged down the ice, and as the puck came to him, he didn't hesitate. He fired a shot past the Bruins' goalie, giving him 10 points—an incredible six goals and four assists in a single game!

The crowd went wild, screaming and cheering louder than ever. Everyone knew they had just witnessed something truly historic. As the final seconds ticked away, Sittler's teammates gathered around him, celebrating not just a win, but one of the greatest individual performances in NHL history. The final score was 11-4 in favor of the Maple Leafs, but the real story was Darryl Sittler's record-breaking 10-point night. It was a performance that left the entire hockey world in awe.

Darryl Sittler's 10-point game was more than just a personal achievement—it was a testament to what can happen when you believe in yourself and play for the team. Sittler didn't go into the game thinking about breaking records. He just wanted to help his team win, and that mindset allowed him to play with freedom and confidence. Sittler's incredible night also showed the power of perseverance. He had faced plenty of challenges throughout his career, including pressure from fans and the media to lead the Leafs to greatness. But Sittler never let that pressure get to him. He focused on working hard, playing his game, and being the best leader he could be for his teammates.

The 10-point game became a symbol of what is possible when preparation meets opportunity. Sittler didn't set out to break records that night, but because of his dedication to his craft, he was ready when the moment came. It's a reminder to always give your best, because you never know when greatness will happen.

Darryl Sittler's 10-point game is a story of hard work, perseverance, and seizing the moment. Even in a sport as tough as hockey, records can be broken if you push yourself beyond what you think is possible. Sittler didn't aim for glory that night, but his passion for the game and his determination to help his team led to one of the most legendary performances in NHL history. Whether you're playing sports, studying for a test, or working toward any goal, remember Darryl Sittler's story. Give your best effort, trust your abilities, and believe that you can achieve something incredible—even if no one expects it. You never know when your own 10-point night might come, and when it does, you'll be ready to make history! (Seide, 2024).

> I never played for the records. I played because I loved the game.
>
> DARRYL SITTLER

CAREER HIGHLIGHTS

- **NHL Debut with the Toronto Maple Leafs**: Selected 8th overall by the Maple Leafs in the 1970 NHL Draft, beginning his iconic career in Toronto.

- **10-Point Game Record**: Set an NHL record by scoring 10 points (6 goals, 4 assists) in a single game against the Boston Bruins on February 7, 1976—a record that still stands today.
- **Back-to-Back Hat Tricks in Playoffs**: Scored a remarkable five goals in a playoff game against the Philadelphia Flyers in 1976, becoming the first player to score back-to-back hat tricks in regular-season and playoff games.
- **Canada Cup Hero**: Scored the series-winning goal in overtime for Team Canada in the 1976 Canada Cup, securing victory against Czechoslovakia and further cementing his legacy.
- **Maple Leafs Captaincy**: Named captain of the Toronto Maple Leafs in 1975, recognized for his leadership and impact on and off the ice.
- **Inducted into the Hockey Hall of Fame**: Honored with induction in 1989, celebrating his contributions to the game and his legendary status.
- **1,000 Points Milestone**: Reached the prestigious 1,000-point mark in his career, joining an elite group of NHL players.
- **Maple Leafs Legend and Icon**: Remains one of the most beloved players in Maple Leafs history, frequently involved with the team and its community.

CHAPTER 6

THE GAME THAT NEVER ENDED

IT WAS THE LONGEST NIGHT IN HOCKEY HISTORY, AND NOBODY knew when it would end. On May 4, 2000, the Philadelphia Flyers and the Pittsburgh Penguins found themselves locked in an epic playoff battle that seemed like it would go on forever. The score was tied 1-1 after three periods, but this was no ordinary game. The clock kept ticking, and period after period passed without a winner. As the game dragged into five overtimes, the players were exhausted, the fans couldn't believe what they were seeing, and the goalies were performing like superheroes. Then, after nearly eight hours of hockey, one player finally ended the marathon. This is the story of the longest NHL playoff game of the modern era—an unbelievable test of endurance, skill, and determination.

KEITH PRIMEAU
"PRIMETIME"
5 OVERTIME GAME WINNER

The year 2000 was a big one for hockey, especially for the Philadelphia Flyers and the Pittsburgh Penguins, two fierce rivals who were facing off in the Eastern Conference Semifinals of the NHL playoffs. These teams didn't like each other, and their games were always intense and hard-fought. Every goal, every hit, and every save mattered as they battled for a chance to move closer to the Stanley Cup.

The Flyers were led by their captain, Eric Lindros, while the Penguins had their superstar forward Jaromir Jagr. Both teams were packed with talent, and this series was expected to be a close one. But no one could have predicted that Game 4 would turn into the longest game of modern NHL history.

Going into the game, the Penguins led the series 2-1. They were hoping to win Game 4 and take a commanding lead in the series. The Flyers, on the other hand, knew they needed a victory to tie the series and keep their Stanley Cup dreams alive. With both teams desperate to win, the game was bound to be a tough fight, but no one could have imagined just how long this battle would last.

The game started like any other, with both teams playing hard and looking for an early advantage. The Penguins struck first, with Alexei Kovalev scoring in the first period to give Pittsburgh a 1-0 lead. The Flyers fought back, and in the second period, John LeClair scored to tie the game at 1-1. The rest of the game was a nail-biter, with both teams creating chances but being stopped by incredible goaltending.

Ron Tugnutt, the Penguins' goalie, and Brian Boucher, the Flyers' rookie netminder, were both playing out of their minds, making save after save to keep the game tied. By the end of the third period, the score was still 1-1, and the game headed into overtime. In the playoffs, overtime is sudden death, which means the first team to score wins the game. But as the first overtime period started, it quickly became clear that neither team was going to give up easily.

Both teams were tired, but the pressure to win kept them pushing. The players skated as hard as they could, even though their legs felt heavy. The coaches made adjustments, trying to find a way to break through the opposing defense. Every shot was met with an incredible save, every chance was blocked by a defender, and the tension in the arena kept growing.

Then the second overtime period started—still no goals. The players were drenched in sweat, breathing hard after hours of nonstop skating. They couldn't rest. They had to keep going, no matter how tired they were. By now, everyone—players, coaches, and fans—knew this game was special. It was turning into an epic battle of endurance and heart.

The third, fourth, and then fifth overtime periods passed, and still, nobody had scored. The game became a test of willpower. Players were exhausted beyond belief, but they had to stay focused. One small mistake could cost their team the game and possibly the series.

Both Ron Tugnutt and Brian Boucher were playing like brick walls in front of the net, refusing to let anything get past them. But everyone wondered, how much longer could they hold out? After five full periods of overtime, both teams were running on fumes. The game had gone on for so long that players were eating energy bars on the bench and drinking gallons of water just to keep going. Some players could barely stand, but no one was willing to quit.

Finally, as the game entered its eighth hour, a play developed that would change everything. Late in the fifth overtime period, Flyers forward Keith Primeau found himself with the puck in the Penguins' zone. Primeau was a strong, experienced player, known for his toughness, but even he was feeling the effects of playing this long, grueling game. Still, he saw an opening. With a quick move, he cut to the middle of the ice and released a perfect wrist shot.

The puck flew through the air toward the Penguins' net. Ron Tugnutt, who had made more than 70 saves by this point, lunged to stop it, but he couldn't get there in time. The puck slid past him and into the net. GOAL! The game was finally over, and the Flyers had won 2-1. Primeau, too tired to even celebrate much, was mobbed by his teammates, who hugged him and patted him on the back. After the longest battle any of them had ever fought, the Flyers were victorious. The moment Keith Primeau's shot hit the back of the net, the arena exploded with cheers.

Fans who had stayed in their seats for hours could hardly believe what they had just witnessed. The longest game in modern NHL history had finally ended, and the Flyers were the winners. It had taken 92 minutes and 1 second of overtime hockey—an entire game's worth of overtime periods.

The players could barely celebrate. They were too exhausted to even raise their sticks in the air. Many of them just collapsed onto the ice, finally able to rest after skating for so long. The goalies, Ron Tugnutt and Brian Boucher, were both praised for their incredible performances. Tugnutt had made 70 saves, while Boucher had stopped 57 shots.

For Keith Primeau, the moment was one of the greatest of his career. He had been battling all game long, just like every other player on the ice, but in the end, he found the strength to make the play that mattered most. His goal ended a game that seemed like it would never end, and it gave the Flyers a crucial win to tie the series at 2-2.

The Flyers and Penguins' five-overtime game was more than just a long hockey game—it was a lesson in perseverance, teamwork, and determination. Both teams pushed themselves to the absolute limit. The players were tired, hurting, and running on empty, but none of them gave up. They knew that their teammates were counting on them, and they kept fighting until the very end.

This game showed everyone that no matter how hard things get, you can always push a little further if you believe in yourself and your team. Whether it's on the ice, in school, or in life, sometimes the biggest challenges require the most effort. The Flyers and Penguins both gave everything they had in that game, and though only one team could win, every player left the ice knowing they had given their all.

Both teams faced incredible challenges during that game, but they kept fighting, shift after shift, period after period. They showed that no matter how tired or overwhelmed you feel, you can always dig deep and find a way to keep going. So, the next time you face a tough situation, whether it's in a game, at school, or in life, remember the Flyers and Penguins from that legendary night. Even when it seems like the challenge will never end, you have the strength to keep pushing forward. Just like in hockey, the greatest victories come from hard work, perseverance, and a belief that you can achieve anything—no matter how long it takes. (Roche, 2024).

> At some point, you just stop thinking about winning or losing. It's about surviving.
>
> BRIAN BOUCHER

CAREER HIGHLIGHTS

Keith Primeau (Flyers)

- **Game-Winning Goal in Five Overtimes**: Scored the game-winning goal after over 92 minutes of overtime, cementing his place in Flyers history.
- **Flyers Captain**: Became captain of the Flyers in 2001, leading with toughness and grit.

Jaromir Jagr (Penguins)

- **Two-Time Stanley Cup Champion**: Won back-to-back Stanley Cups with the Penguins in 1991 and 1992.
- **Art Ross Trophy Wins**: Captured the Art Ross Trophy five times as the league's leading scorer.
- **Longevity in the NHL**: Played over 1,700 games across three decades, making him one of the longest-tenured players in NHL history.

Brian Boucher (Flyers, Goaltender)

- **Record-Breaking Shutout Streak**: Set an NHL record for the longest shutout streak by a rookie, with five consecutive shutouts in 2004.

- **Clutch Performance in Five-Overtime Game**: Made 57 saves in the marathon game against the Penguins, helping keep the Flyers in contention.

Andy Delmore (Flyers)

- **Two Goals in Five-Overtime Game**: Scored two goals in the five-overtime game, including the tying goal that sent the game to overtime.
- **Playoff Heroics**: Known for scoring key goals in the playoffs, including a hat trick against the Penguins in the same series.

Alexei Kovalev (Penguins)

- **Stanley Cup Champion**: Won the Stanley Cup with the New York Rangers in 1994.
- **International Success**: Represented Russia in multiple international tournaments, winning gold in the 1992 Winter Olympics.
- **1,000-Point Milestone**: Finished his career with over 1,000 NHL points, solidifying his status as one of the top Russian players in league history.

CHAPTER 7
THE LEGENDARY CAREER OF MR. HOCKEY

IMAGINE A HOCKEY PLAYER SO GREAT THAT PEOPLE START calling him "Mr. Hockey." That player was Gordie Howe, and he didn't just dominate the game for a few years—he ruled the ice for decades. Howe's incredible career spanned five different decades, and he wasn't just known for his scoring ability, but also for his toughness and leadership. Whether it was scoring goals or making plays, Howe did it all. With over 800 goals, four Stanley Cups, and a reputation for being one of the toughest players ever, Gordie Howe's career was one of the greatest in sports history. But how did this small-town boy become a legend?

GORDIE HOWE
"MR. HOCKEY"
5-DECADE HOCKEY CAREER!

Gordie Howe was born in Floral, Saskatchewan, Canada, in 1928, and like many Canadian kids, he grew up playing hockey on frozen ponds. From an early age, Howe stood out—not just because of his size and strength, but because of his love for the game. Even as a boy, he was a natural. He could skate faster, shoot harder, and hit tougher than anyone else his age. Howe's journey to hockey greatness wasn't an easy one. As a young boy, his family didn't have much money, so Howe practiced with homemade equipment and worn-out skates. But none of that stopped him. He was determined to play hockey at the highest level, and by the time he was a teenager, he had caught the attention of NHL scouts.

At just 18 years old, Howe joined the Detroit Red Wings in 1946. Right from the start, he made an impact. He wasn't just a goal scorer—he was a complete player, combining his physical play with smart decisions on the ice. By his second season, everyone in the league knew that Gordie Howe was something special. But even with all of his early success, no one could have predicted just how long and successful his career would be.

Gordie Howe's career wasn't without challenges. Although he was a superstar from the beginning, hockey in the 1940s and 1950s was a rough, physical game. Howe had to constantly prove himself against tough competition, and injuries were always a risk.

In 1950, just four years into his NHL career, Howe suffered a serious head injury during a playoff game against the Toronto Maple Leafs. He was chasing a puck near the boards when he collided with an opponent, causing him to fall headfirst into the boards. The impact was so severe that Howe had to undergo emergency surgery to save his life.

Many people thought that Howe's career might be over. The injury was serious, and doctors weren't sure if he would ever play hockey again. But Gordie Howe wasn't someone who gave up easily. Not only did he recover, but he came back stronger than ever. The very next season, he led the NHL in scoring and helped the Red Wings win the Stanley Cup.

Over the next decade, Howe established himself as the best player in hockey. He won the Hart Trophy (given to the league's most valuable player) six times and led the Red Wings to four Stanley Cup championships. But Howe wasn't just known for his skill—he was also known for his toughness. If an opponent tried anything funny with him or his teammates, Howe wouldn't hesitate to drop the gloves and defend himself. This combination of skill and toughness became known as the "Gordie Howe Hat Trick"—scoring a goal, getting an assist, and getting into a fight, all in the same game.

But the biggest challenge for Howe came not from injuries or opponents, but from the passage of time. As the years went by, Howe kept playing, even as he got older. Most players retire in their 30s, but not Gordie Howe.

He continued to compete at a high level well into his 40s and eventually made a historic return to the ice in his 50s. The game kept changing, but Howe always found a way to keep up.

By the late 1960s, Gordie Howe had already achieved everything a player could dream of. He had set records, won championships, and become a hockey legend. But in 1971, at age 43, Howe decided to retire from the NHL. His body was feeling the effects of over two decades of professional hockey, and he thought it was time to hang up his skates. However, retirement didn't last long for Gordie Howe. After a couple of years away from the game, he started feeling the itch to play again. His two sons, Mark and Marty Howe, were playing in the World Hockey Association (WHA), a rival league to the NHL, and Gordie saw an opportunity to do something that had never been done before: play professional hockey along-side his sons.

In 1973, Howe made a stunning comeback, joining the Houston Aeros of the WHA. At the age of 45, Howe was not only able to keep up with younger players, but he thrived. In his first season back, he scored 31 goals and led the Aeros to the WHA Championship. It was a remarkable comeback, and playing with his sons made it even more special. The Howes became the first father-son trio to play on the same profes-sional hockey team.

This moment marked a new chapter in Howe's career. Instead of being remembered as a player who dominated just one league, he became known as a player who could compete at a high level no matter the circumstances. He wasn't just a star in the NHL—he was a star in any league he played in.

The peak of Gordie Howe's career came not in a single game, but in the fact that he played at such a high level for so long. His ability to compete at the highest level into his 50s was unheard of. After dominating the WHA for several years, Howe made another surprising move: he returned to the NHL. In 1979, at age 51, Howe joined the Hartford Whalers, who had just merged into the NHL from the WHA. Most players never get close to playing in their 50s, but Howe wasn't just playing—he was contributing. In his final NHL season, Howe played all 80 regular-season games and scored 15 goals. He wasn't just a player filling a roster spot; he was a key part of the team, showing younger players what it meant to be a true professional.

One of the most memorable moments of his final season came during the 1979 NHL All-Star Game. At age 51, Howe was selected to play in the game, and the fans gave him a standing ovation. It was a fitting tribute to a player who had given so much to the game for so many years. Even at that advanced age, Howe skated alongside the best players in the world and held his own.

When Howe finally retired for good in 1980, his career stats were staggering: over 800 goals, more than 1,800 points, and four Stanley Cups. He had played in five different decades, something no one had ever done before or since. His career was a testament to his skill, toughness, and incredible longevity.

Gordie Howe's career is one of the most inspiring in all of sports. He wasn't just a great hockey player—he was someone who showed that hard work, determination, and a love for the game can carry you to incredible heights. Even when he faced injuries, age, or doubt from others, Howe never backed down. He loved hockey, and that passion kept him going for more than 30 years.

One of the biggest lessons from Howe's career is that success isn't just about talent—it's about perseverance. Howe didn't let challenges stop him, and he didn't let anyone tell him he was too old to keep playing. He set records not just because he was talented, but because he outworked everyone around him. His story is a reminder that no matter what obstacles you face, you can achieve greatness if you put in the effort.

Gordie Howe is proof that there are no limits to what you can accomplish if you have determination, toughness, and a love for what you do. Whether you're a hockey player or chasing a different dream, you can learn from Howe's example. He didn't let age, injuries, or competition hold him back.

Instead, he pushed himself to be the best for as long as he could, and in the process, became a legend. So, the next time you're facing a challenge, remember Gordie Howe. Whether it's a tough game, a big test, or a goal you've been working toward, you have the power to overcome it. Just like Howe, you can set records, break barriers, and achieve your dreams. Keep working hard, stay focused, and believe in yourself. With that mindset, anything is possible—even playing professional hockey for five decades, just like "Mr. Hockey" himself! (Hub, 2024).

> You've got to love what you're doing. If you love it, you can overcome any handicap or the soreness or all the aches and pains.
>
> GORDIE HOWE

CAREER HIGHLIGHTS

- **NHL Debut and Early Success**: Made his NHL debut with the Detroit Red Wings in 1946 at just 18 years old, immediately showcasing his talent and toughness.
- **Four-Time Stanley Cup Champion**: Won four Stanley Cups with the Detroit Red Wings (1950, 1952, 1954, 1955), cementing his place as a champion.

- **Six-Time Hart Trophy Winner**: Awarded the Hart Trophy as the NHL's Most Valuable Player six times (1952, 1953, 1957, 1958, 1960, 1963), recognizing his dominance on the ice.
- **Six-Time Art Ross Trophy Winner**: Led the NHL in points six times, earning the Art Ross Trophy (1951, 1952, 1953, 1954, 1957, 1963) as the league's top scorer.
- **First Player to Score 1,000 Points**: Became the first player in NHL history to reach 1,000 career points, setting a new standard for excellence.
- **Played in Five Different Decades**: His career spanned from the 1940s to the 1980s, an incredible five decades, playing his final NHL game at 52 years old with the Hartford Whalers in 1980.
- **1,767 NHL Games Played**: Set an NHL record for games played at 1,767, showcasing his incredible longevity and durability.
- **Hall of Fame Induction**: Inducted into the Hockey Hall of Fame in 1972, solidifying his legacy as one of the greatest players of all time.

CHAPTER 8
JIM KYTE MAKES NHL HISTORY

Imagine playing in the National Hockey League (NHL), where communication on the ice is key—players call for passes, coaches shout instructions, and the roar of the crowd is deafening. Now, imagine doing all of that without being able to hear. This was the challenge that Jim Kyte faced, yet he defied the odds to become the first, and so far only, legally deaf player in NHL history. Kyte's determination and resilience not only helped him achieve his dreams but also inspired countless others to believe that nothing is impossible. This is the story of how Jim Kyte broke barriers and made history in the world of hockey.

JIM KYTE
"GENTLEMAN JIM"
NHL'S FIRST DEAF PLAYER

Jim Kyte was born in Ottawa, Ontario, Canada in 1964 into a family that was no stranger to challenges. Jim and his four brothers were all born with a genetic condition called hereditary deafness, meaning they were either born deaf or experienced significant hearing loss. From a young age, Jim was fitted with hearing aids, and while he couldn't hear as well as other kids, he didn't let that stop him from pursuing his love of hockey. Growing up, Jim dreamed of playing in the NHL just like many Canadian kids. He practiced hard, developing his skills as a defenseman and learning how to adapt to his hearing loss on the ice.

Kyte had to rely on visual cues and his sense of awareness to read the play since he couldn't hear the sounds of skates cutting the ice, pucks hitting sticks, or teammates calling out for passes. But instead of seeing his hearing impairment as a barrier, Jim used it as motivation to work even harder.

Kyte's talent and determination paid off. After excelling in junior hockey with the Winnipeg Warriors of the Western Hockey League (WHL), Jim was selected 12th overall by the Winnipeg Jets in the 1982 NHL Entry Draft. He had accomplished something incredible—he was on his way to becoming the first deaf player in NHL history. Being legally deaf in a fast-paced, highly competitive sport like hockey presented Jim Kyte with a unique set of challenges. While other players could rely on hearing their coaches or teammates, Jim had to depend on what he could see and feel on the ice.

Communication with his teammates became crucial, and Kyte developed a special system with his fellow players, using hand signals and reading lips to understand what was happening in real time. But the challenges didn't stop there. Kyte had to wear hearing aids off the ice, but because hockey is such a physical game, he couldn't wear them while playing. This meant that during games, he was operating in near silence. On top of that, being a physical defenseman meant Jim often found himself in scrappy situations, delivering big hits and sometimes dropping the gloves in fights to protect his teammates. He couldn't hear the referee's whistle to stop play or the noise of the crowd, so he had to stay alert and always be ready for anything.

Off the ice, Jim faced skepticism from some people who doubted whether a deaf player could truly succeed in the NHL. But Kyte wasn't one to let doubters hold him back. Instead, he embraced the challenge and proved that with the right mindset and determination, he could play at the highest level of hockey, just like anyone else.

Kyte's determination to succeed reached a turning point when he made his NHL debut with the Winnipeg Jets in 1983. Not only was he fulfilling his childhood dream of playing in the NHL, but he was also breaking new ground as the first deaf player to ever skate in the league. His presence on the ice was more than just a personal achievement—it was a statement that physical limitations didn't have to define a person's potential.

Kyte's work ethic quickly earned him the respect of his teammates and coaches. As a defenseman, he was known for his toughness and willingness to stand up for his team. He wasn't the most skilled player, but he made up for it with his grit and determination. His ability to adapt to the game despite his hearing loss showed that he was not only capable of competing in the NHL but also of thriving in it.

One key moment that solidified Kyte's role in the league came when he scored his first NHL goal. It wasn't just a milestone for him—it was proof that he belonged in the NHL and that his hard work had paid off. Over the course of his career, Kyte would go on to play more than 600 games in the NHL, proving his doubters wrong time and time again. Kyte's NHL career spanned from 1983 to 1997, during which he played for several teams, including the Winnipeg Jets, Pittsburgh Penguins, Calgary Flames, Ottawa Senators, and San Jose Sharks. His journey was filled with memorable moments, but perhaps the most significant was his role as an ambassador for deaf and hearing-impaired athletes.

Throughout his career, Kyte used his platform to inspire others who faced similar challenges. He showed young athletes with disabilities that they, too, could achieve their dreams, no matter what obstacles stood in their way.

Kyte became a symbol of perseverance, not only in the hockey community but also beyond. On the ice, he was known for his physical play and his commitment to his teammates. He wasn't afraid to throw big hits or get into tough situations, and he gained a reputation as a reliable defenseman who could be counted on when it mattered most. While he never won the Stanley Cup, Kyte's career was marked by his resilience and ability to overcome adversity.

As the first deaf player in the NHL, Kyte opened the door for other athletes with disabilities to pursue their dreams in professional sports. He didn't just make history for himself—he paved the way for others to follow in his footsteps.

Jim Kyte's story is one of courage, perseverance, and determination. He faced challenges that most hockey players never have to deal with, but instead of letting his hearing loss stop him, he used it as motivation to work even harder. Kyte proved that physical limitations don't define a person's potential. Instead, it's the heart, passion, and dedication to the game that truly matter.

Kyte's journey to becoming the first deaf player in NHL history shows that with the right mindset and support, anything is possible. His success was not just about his talent as a hockey player but also about his resilience in the face of adversity. He proved that if you work hard and believe in yourself, you can break down barriers and achieve greatness, no matter the odds. (Cowley, 2021).

It's not about what you can't do; it's about what you can do.

JIM KYTE

CAREER HIGHLIGHT

- **First Legally Deaf Player in NHL History**: Broke barriers as the first and, to date, only legally deaf player in the NHL, paving the way for greater inclusion in professional sports.
- **Drafted by the Winnipeg Jets**: Selected 12th overall in the 1982 NHL Draft by the Winnipeg Jets, marking a significant achievement as a high draft pick and promising defenseman.
- **Ten-Year NHL Career**: Played 598 NHL games over ten seasons with teams including the Winnipeg Jets, Pittsburgh Penguins, Calgary Flames, Ottawa Senators, and San Jose Sharks.
- **Physical, Gritty Style of Play**: Known for his tough, physical presence on the ice, Kyte was a dependable enforcer and a respected team player.
- **Advocate for Disability Awareness**: Used his platform to advocate for the deaf and hard-of-hearing community, inspiring others with disabilities to pursue their dreams.

- **Inducted into the Canadian Disability Hall of Fame**: Recognized for his achievements and contributions to disability awareness and inclusion in sports.

CHAPTER 9
THE 44-YEAR-OLD GOALIE WHO SAVED THE DAY

IMAGINE BEING IN THE MIDDLE OF A HEATED PLAYOFF GAME when your team's goalie gets injured, and there's no backup available. What would you do? For the New York Rangers, that nightmare became a reality during the 1928 Stanley Cup Finals. But instead of panicking, something incredible happened. Lester Patrick, the Rangers' 44-year-old coach, decided to suit up as goalie and save his team. That's right—Patrick, who hadn't played in years, put on the pads and stepped between the pipes in one of the most dramatic moments in hockey history. What unfolded that night was a story of bravery, determination, and one of the most legendary moments in NHL history. But how did a coach end up making one of the greatest saves in Stanley Cup history?

LESTER PATRICK
"THE SILVER FOX"
THE COACH WHO BECAME A GOALIE

Lester Patrick was no stranger to hockey greatness. Born in Drummondville, Quebec, in 1883, Patrick grew up in a time when hockey was just starting to become organized. From a young age, he and his brother Frank Patrick were known as pioneers of the game, helping to shape hockey into the sport we know today. Lester was a skilled defenseman who played for several teams during the early 1900s, but by the 1920s, he had retired from playing and taken on the role of coach and general manager of the New York Rangers. Under Patrick's leadership, the Rangers quickly became one of the best teams in the NHL, even though they were a relatively new franchise, having joined the league in 1926. Patrick's knowledge of the game, combined with his innovative ideas, made him one of the smartest hockey minds of his time.

But no one could have expected that during the 1928 Stanley Cup Finals, he would go from coaching behind the bench to playing in goal. The Rangers were up against the Montreal Maroons in the Stanley Cup Finals, a tough team with plenty of talent. It was Game 2 of the series, and the Rangers were trailing 1-0 in the series after losing Game 1. They couldn't afford to lose again, but something unthinkable happened early in the game that would force Patrick to take matters into his own hands. The Rangers' starting goalie, Lorne Chabot, was one of the best netminders in the league. But in the first period of Game 2, he was hit in the face by a puck and suffered a serious eye injury.

With no protective masks at the time, goalies often faced dangerous situations, and Chabot's injury was severe enough that he couldn't continue playing. Suddenly, the Rangers were without a goalie, and the game was still in progress.

In today's NHL, teams have backup goalies ready to step in when needed, but back in 1928, things were different. The Rangers didn't have a backup goalie on the roster. As Chabot was being taken to the hospital, the Rangers faced a difficult situation—without a goalie, they couldn't continue the game. The team scrambled to find a solution. At first, they tried to borrow the Maroons' backup goalie, but the Maroons refused, leaving the Rangers with no choice but to look for someone within their own ranks. That's when Lester Patrick, the team's coach and general manager, made a bold decision: he would put on the goalie pads and finish the game himself. At 44 years old, Patrick hadn't played in goal at a professional level, and he hadn't played any hockey in several years. But with no other options, Patrick took a deep breath and prepared for one of the most incredible moments in hockey history.

The sight of 44-year-old Lester Patrick stepping onto the ice in full goalie gear was something no one in the arena could believe. Patrick had been a great player in his day, but he was a defenseman, not a goaltender. His decision to play in goal was risky, but it was the only chance the Rangers had to keep their Stanley Cup dreams alive.

As Patrick took his place in net, the Rangers rallied around their coach. They knew they had to protect him as much as possible, blocking shots and playing tight defense to prevent the Maroons from getting too many chances. The crowd in Montreal Forum couldn't believe what they were seeing—a coach, well past his playing days, now standing between the pipes in a Stanley Cup Final game. The odds were against him, but Patrick was determined to prove that he could still compete.

The Maroons quickly tried to take advantage of the situation. They launched shot after shot at Patrick, testing the 44-year-old's reflexes and nerves. But Patrick held his ground. Time and again, he made saves, using his instincts and hockey knowledge to stop the puck. His style wasn't pretty—after all, he wasn't a real goalie—but it worked. He blocked shots with his body, his stick, and his skates, doing whatever he could to keep the puck out of the net.

As the minutes ticked away, something incredible started to happen. The Rangers gained confidence, knowing their coach was holding his own in goal. They started attacking more, looking for a chance to score and win the game for their fearless leader. With the game tied at 1-1 and heading into overtime, the tension in the arena was at an all-time high. Both teams knew that the next goal would be critical, but for the Rangers, the pressure was even greater.

Their coach was in goal, and they were fighting to even the series and keep their championship hopes alive. The overtime period was intense, with both teams fighting for every inch of the ice. The Maroons tried to test Patrick with more shots, but he continued to make saves, defying the odds with each stop. Then, suddenly, the Rangers got their chance. After a scramble in front of the Maroons' net, Rangers forward Frank Boucher found the puck and buried it in the back of the net. GOAL! The Rangers had won the game 2-1 in overtime, and their coach, Lester Patrick, had just made one of the most improbable appearances in Stanley Cup history. As the players celebrated, they lifted Patrick onto their shoulders, cheering for the man who had saved their season.

The victory wasn't just a win for the Rangers—it was a legendary moment that would be remembered forever. Patrick had stepped up when his team needed him most, and against all odds, he had led them to victory.

Lester Patrick's incredible decision to play goalie in the Stanley Cup Finals showed the world what true leadership and bravery look like. He didn't have to step onto the ice that night, but he knew his team needed him, and he wasn't about to let them down. Even though he hadn't played in years and had never been a goaltender, Patrick took on the challenge, and in doing so, he showed that anything is possible when you're willing to step up and face adversity head-on.

Patrick's courage and determination inspired not only his team but the entire hockey world. His willingness to do whatever it took to help the Rangers win showed that great leaders lead by example, even when the odds are against them. For the Rangers, the win was about more than just tying the series—it was about believing in themselves and their coach. The Rangers would go on to win the Stanley Cup that year, and while Patrick didn't play in goal again, his heroic performance in Game 2 became the stuff of legend.

Lester Patrick's story is a reminder that you never know when you'll be called upon to do something extraordinary. Sometimes, you'll face challenges that seem impossible, but if you believe in yourself and are willing to take risks, you can overcome even the toughest obstacles. Patrick's bravery, stepping into an unfamiliar role to help his team, teaches us that true leaders don't shy away from challenges—they face them head-on. Whether you're playing sports, tackling a tough project, or facing any kind of challenge, remember Lester Patrick's incredible night in goal. Even when the odds are stacked against you, you can achieve great things if you're willing to step up and give it your all. So, the next time you're faced with a challenge, think of Lester Patrick and know that with courage and determination, you can accomplish anything—even becoming a hero at 44 years old! (Anderson, 2019).

The strength of a team lies in the hearts of the players, not in the numbers on the scoreboard.

LESTER PATRICK

CAREER HIGHLIGHTS

- **Early Playing Career**: Played as a defenseman in the early 1900s, known for his toughness and skill, making him one of the first true stars in professional hockey.
- **Innovator of the Sport**: Credited with numerous innovations, including the use of blue lines to divide the rink into zones and the development of the forward pass, which transformed hockey into a faster-paced game.
- **Stanley Cup Champion as a Player**: Won two Stanley Cups as a player with the Montreal Wanderers (1906) and the Victoria Aristocrats (1925), showcasing his talent on the ice.
- **Coach and General Manager of the New York Rangers**: Became head coach and general manager of the New York Rangers in 1926, leading the team to early success and building them into a competitive franchise.
- **Stanley Cup Champion as a Coach**: Coached the New York Rangers to two Stanley Cup

championships (1928 and 1933), solidifying his place as a successful and resourceful leader.

- **Hockey Hall of Fame Induction**: Inducted into the Hockey Hall of Fame in 1947, recognizing his lasting impact and legacy on the game.

CHAPTER 10
OVERTIME WINNER ON A BROKEN ANKLE

IMAGINE BEING IN THE MOST IMPORTANT GAME OF YOUR LIFE, with your team on the verge of elimination, and suddenly you're hit with a devastating injury. Most players would leave the game, but not Bob Baun. During Game 6 of the 1964 Stanley Cup Finals, Baun, a tough defenseman for the Toronto Maple Leafs, suffered a broken ankle. Everyone assumed he was done for the night. But incredibly, Baun not only returned to the game, he did the unthinkable—he scored the game-winning goal in overtime, keeping his team's championship hopes alive. It was one of the most legendary moments in hockey history, proving that heart and determination can overcome even the most painful obstacles. But how did Baun find the strength to keep playing, let alone score the winning goal?

BOB BAUN
"BOOMER"
GAME WINNER ON A
BROKEN ANKLE

Bob Baun grew up in a small town in Lanigan, Saskatchewan, where hockey was more than just a game—it was a way of life. From a young age, Baun learned the value of hard work, toughness, and dedication. He wasn't the biggest or fastest player on the ice, but he made up for it with his grit and determination. Baun's path to the National Hockey League (NHL) wasn't easy, but his relentless work ethic helped him earn a spot with the Toronto Maple Leafs in 1956.

As a defenseman, Baun was known for his physical play and willingness to block shots. He wasn't a flashy player, but he was the kind of teammate every team needed—someone who would do whatever it took to help his team win. By the time the 1964 Stanley Cup Finals rolled around, Baun had earned a reputation as one of the toughest defensemen in the league. The Leafs had already won back-to-back Stanley Cups in 1962 and 1963, and they were looking for a third. But in 1964, they faced a fierce battle against the Detroit Red Wings, and the series had turned into a grueling fight.

Heading into Game 6, the Red Wings led the series 3-2, meaning the Leafs had to win or their season would be over. The pressure was on, and Baun and his teammates knew they had to give everything they had. Little did they know, this game would become one of the most unforgettable moments in NHL history.

The 1964 Stanley Cup Finals between the Maple Leafs and the Red Wings was a hard-fought series. Both teams were evenly matched, and every game was a battle. Game 6 was no different. The Red Wings had a chance to close out the series and win the Stanley Cup on their home ice in Detroit. The Leafs, on the other hand, were playing for their season. They knew that a loss would mean the end of their championship dreams.

Bob Baun, as always, was playing his usual tough, physical game. He was blocking shots, delivering hits, and doing everything he could to keep the Red Wings from scoring. But late in the third period, disaster struck. Baun went down to block a shot from Gordie Howe, one of the most dangerous players in the league. As the puck hit Baun's ankle, he immediately knew something was wrong. The pain was sharp, and he couldn't put any weight on his leg. He was helped off the ice and taken to the locker room.

It was clear that Baun had suffered a serious injury, and most people thought his night was over. The Leafs needed every player at full strength if they were going to win, and losing Baun was a huge blow. With the game tied 3-3 and heading into overtime, the Leafs were facing the possibility of losing the Stanley Cup without one of their key defensemen. But Baun wasn't ready to give up.

As Baun sat in the locker room, he was told that he had likely broken his ankle. For most players, that would have been the end of their night, but Baun wasn't like most players.

He knew his team needed him, and he wasn't about to let them down. Despite the pain, Baun made a decision that would change the course of the game—he was going back in. Baun had his ankle taped up tightly, and with the help of some painkillers, he hobbled back to the bench. His teammates couldn't believe it. How could Baun possibly play on a broken ankle? But when they saw the determination in his eyes, they knew he was serious. Baun wasn't just going to sit on the bench—he was going to make a difference.

When overtime started, the tension in the arena was palpable. Every play, every shot, and every hit could be the one that decided the game. The Red Wings were pressing hard, looking for the goal that would end the series and win them the Stanley Cup. But the Leafs, inspired by Baun's courage, were determined to fight back. Then came the moment that would make Bob Baun a legend. Early in overtime, the Leafs won a faceoff in the Red Wings' zone, and the puck came to Baun at the blue line. Without hesitating, Baun took a shot. It wasn't the hardest shot of his career, but it was accurate. The puck sailed through traffic and found its way past Terry Sawchuk, the Red Wings' goalie.

GOAL! The Leafs had won the game 4-3, forcing a Game 7 in the series. The crowd erupted, and Baun's teammates mobbed him in celebration. But while the team celebrated, Baun could barely stand. His ankle was throbbing, but in that moment, none of that mattered.

He had just scored the game-winning goal in overtime on a broken ankle, keeping the Leafs' championship hopes alive. The victory was more than just a win for the Maple Leafs—it was a moment of pure determination and courage. Baun's willingness to play through the pain and deliver the game-winning goal was a testament to his toughness and heart. It was a moment that hockey fans would talk about for years to come.

After the game, Baun was taken to the hospital, where X-rays confirmed what everyone had suspected—his ankle was indeed broken. But the Maple Leafs still had one more game to play. Just two days later, the Leafs and Red Wings faced off in Game 7 in Toronto. Baun, despite his injury, insisted on playing again. The Leafs, inspired by his courage, played their hearts out and won Game 7 by a score of 4-0, capturing the Stanley Cup.

Bob Baun's incredible performance in Game 6 showed the world what true toughness and dedication look like. His willingness to play through a broken ankle to help his team win is one of the most remarkable displays of courage in sports history. For Baun, it wasn't just about being tough—it was about doing whatever it took to help his team succeed. The lesson from Baun's heroic moment is clear: no matter how difficult the situation, if you believe in yourself and are willing to push through the pain, you can achieve incredible things.

Bob Baun's story is one of courage, toughness, and an unshakable belief in the power of teamwork. When most players would have left the game due to injury, Baun chose to fight through the pain for the sake of his team. His decision to return to the ice and score the game-winning goal on a broken ankle showed that with determination and heart, anything is possible. The next time you face a challenge, whether in sports, school, or life, remember Bob Baun's legendary moment. Even when things seem impossible, you have the strength to push through and achieve greatness. If Baun could score the game-winning goal on a broken ankle, imagine what you can do with hard work, perseverance, and a never-give-up attitude. Keep pushing forward, and you too can make history!

(Davidson, 2023).

Pain never entered my mind. All I wanted was to be out there helping my team.

BOB BAUN

CAREER HIGHLIGHTS

- **NHL Debut with the Toronto Maple Leafs**: Made his NHL debut in 1956 with the Maple Leafs, quickly establishing himself as a dependable, hard-hitting defenseman.

- **Four-Time Stanley Cup Champion**: Won four Stanley Cups with the Toronto Maple Leafs (1962, 1963, 1964, 1967), contributing to one of the most successful eras in team history.
- **The Legendary "Broken Ankle" Game**: In Game 6 of the 1964 Stanley Cup Finals, Baun famously returned to the ice after breaking his ankle, scoring the game-winning goal in overtime to keep the Leafs' championship hopes alive. Toronto went on to win the Cup in Game 7.
- **Known for Physical Play**: Developed a reputation as one of the toughest defensemen of his time, known for blocking shots and delivering hard hits to opponents.
- **Long NHL Career**: Played a total of 17 seasons in the NHL, primarily with the Maple Leafs, but also had stints with the Detroit Red Wings and Oakland Seals.
- **NHL All-Star**: Selected to play in the NHL All-Star Game, recognizing his skill and impact as a defenseman.

CHAPTER 11
FIVE CHAMPIONSHIPS IN-A-ROW

It was the spring of 1960, and the Montreal Canadiens were on the verge of making history. They had already won the Stanley Cup four years in a row—an incredible feat that few teams could even dream of achieving. But the Canadiens weren't done yet. They were looking to do something no other team had ever done: win the Stanley Cup for the fifth straight year. With legends like Maurice "Rocket" Richard, Jean Béliveau, and Jacques Plante leading the charge, the Canadiens were ready to cement their place as the greatest hockey dynasty of all time. This is the story of how the Montreal Canadiens became five-time champions, a record that still stands to this day.

MAURICE RICHARD
"ROCKET"
STAR PLAYER ON
THE MONTREAL
5-IN-A-ROW
TEAM

The Montreal Canadiens have always been one of the most successful and famous teams in hockey. By the time the 1950s came around, they were already known as a powerhouse. Coached by Toe Blake, the Canadiens were full of star players like Maurice Richard, a dangerous goal scorer, and Jean Béliveau, their brilliant captain. But perhaps their most important player was goaltender Jacques Plante, whose innovative style and incredible reflexes made him one of the best netminders in the world.

Starting in 1956, the Canadiens began a stretch of dominance that would change the NHL forever. They won the Stanley Cup in 1956, 1957, 1958, and 1959, defeating every challenger that stood in their way. By 1960, Montreal was aiming for its fifth consecutive Cup, a feat that no team in hockey had ever accomplished. But winning five straight championships wasn't going to be easy. The league was filled with tough teams, and every opponent wanted to be the one to stop Montreal's historic run. The pressure was on for the Canadiens to prove that they were still the best, and with their older players like Maurice Richard nearing the end of their careers, this might be their last chance to make history.

Winning one Stanley Cup is hard enough, but winning five in a row? That takes something truly special. The Canadiens were feeling the weight of the challenge, knowing that everyone in the league wanted to see them fail.

Teams like the Toronto Maple Leafs and the Chicago Blackhawks were desperate to dethrone Montreal and take their place as Stanley Cup champions. Montreal's players knew that the 1959-60 season would be a grind. Maurice Richard, who had been the face of the franchise for years, was 38 years old and nearing the end of his legendary career. But even though the Rocket wasn't as fast as he once was, he still had the heart of a champion. Jean Béliveau, on the other hand, was in his prime, and he took on the role of team leader, making sure that the Canadiens stayed focused and hungry for victory.

In goal, Jacques Plante was as sharp as ever. Plante had already revolutionized the game by becoming the first goalie to wear a mask, and he continued to make game-saving stops when his team needed him most. But the pressure of winning five straight Cups wasn't just on the stars—it was on every player. The Canadiens had to play as a team and rely on each other if they wanted to complete their historic run. As the playoffs approached, the Canadiens knew they had to bring their best. Every game was a battle, and they couldn't afford to let their guard down for even a moment.

The 1960 Stanley Cup playoffs started with the Canadiens facing their arch-rivals, the Chicago Blackhawks, in the semifinals. The Blackhawks were one of the toughest teams in the league, with stars like Bobby Hull and Stan Mikita leading the way.

But the Canadiens were determined to keep their dynasty alive. Led by Jean Béliveau's leadership and Jacques Plante's incredible goaltending, Montreal swept the Blackhawks in four straight games, advancing to the Stanley Cup Finals.

Now, just one opponent stood in their way: the Toronto Maple Leafs. The Leafs were a young, hungry team with a lot of talent. They had watched Montreal win four straight championships and were eager to stop them from winning a fifth. But the Canadiens, fueled by their desire to make history, played some of their best hockey of the season. In Game 1 of the Finals, Montreal dominated Toronto, winning 4-2. The Canadiens followed that up with a 2-1 victory in Game 2, taking a commanding lead in the series.

With two more wins, the Canadiens could become five-time champions. The pressure was immense, but Montreal thrived under pressure.

By the time Game 4 arrived, the Canadiens had a chance to sweep the series and win the Stanley Cup for the fifth consecutive year. The atmosphere in the arena was electric, with fans eagerly anticipating the chance to witness history. The game was fast-paced and physical, with both teams giving everything they had. Toronto fought hard, determined to avoid a sweep, but Montreal's experience and skill were too much to overcome.

Late in the game, the Canadiens took control. Maurice Richard, in one of the final games of his career, scored a goal that sent the crowd into a frenzy. It was a fitting moment for the Rocket, who had given so much to the Canadiens over the years. Jean Béliveau added another goal, sealing the victory for Montreal.

When the final buzzer sounded, the Canadiens had won 4-0, completing the sweep of the Maple Leafs and capturing their fifth straight Stanley Cup. The players jumped off the bench, celebrating on the ice as the fans cheered wildly. Maurice Richard raised his arms in triumph, knowing that this was the perfect way to end his career. Jacques Plante, who had been a rock in goal throughout the series, was mobbed by his teammates. It was a moment of pure joy and celebration. The Montreal Canadiens had done the impossible—they had won the Stanley Cup five years in a row, a record that has never been matched.

Over the course of five seasons, Montreal faced countless challenges. They played through injuries, dealt with pressure from fans and media, and fought off tough opponents. But through it all, they stayed focused on their goal. The Canadiens showed that greatness isn't just about winning once—it's about consistently working hard, even when you're already on top. Their five straight Stanley Cups were a testament to their ability to push themselves to be the best, year after year.

This story teaches us the power of perseverance. Even when you've already achieved great things, there's always more to accomplish if you're willing to keep pushing and challenging yourself. The Canadiens' dynasty remains one of the greatest in sports history because they never settled for anything less than their best. (Whitten, 2016).

> Talent is a gift, but you can only succeed with hard work.
>
> JEAN BÉLIVEAU

CAREER HIGHLIGHTS

Maurice "Rocket" Richard (Right Wing)

- **First Player to Score 500 Goals**: Achieved the milestone as the first player in NHL history to score 500 career goals.
- **Eight-Time Stanley Cup Champion**: Won eight Stanley Cups with the Canadiens, including the five consecutive championships.
- **Namesake of the Maurice "Rocket" Richard Trophy**: Honored with a trophy named after him, awarded annually to the league's top goal scorer.

Jean Béliveau (Center)

- **Ten-Time Stanley Cup Champion**: Won a total of 10 Stanley Cups in his career, the most by any player with a single team.
- **Two-Time Hart Trophy Winner**: Recognized as the NHL's Most Valuable Player in 1956 and 1964.
- **Hockey Hall of Fame Inductee**: Inducted into the Hockey Hall of Fame in 1972, recognized for his skill, leadership, and class on and off the ice.

Doug Harvey (Defenseman)

- **Seven-Time Norris Trophy Winner**: Dominated as the NHL's best defenseman, winning the Norris Trophy seven times throughout his career.
- **Nine-Time Stanley Cup Champion**: Won nine Stanley Cups, eight with the Canadiens and one with the New York Rangers.
- **Hockey Hall of Fame Inductee**: Inducted into the Hall of Fame in 1973 for his contributions to the game.

Bernie "Boom Boom" Geoffrion (Right Wing)

- **Inventor of the Slapshot**: Popularized the slapshot, adding a new, powerful weapon to the offensive side of hockey.

- **Two-Time Art Ross Trophy Winner**: Led the league in points twice, proving his skill as both a goal scorer and playmaker.
- **Six-Time Stanley Cup Champion**: Played a crucial role in the Canadiens' five consecutive championships and added another in 1966.
- **Inducted into the Hockey Hall of Fame**: Honored in 1972 for his skill, innovation, and impact on the game.

Jacques Plante (Goaltender)

- **Innovative Goalie Mask**: First goalie to regularly wear a mask in games, revolutionizing safety in the position.
- **Six-Time Vezina Trophy Winner**: Won the Vezina Trophy as the NHL's best goaltender six times.
- **Seven-Time Stanley Cup Champion**: Backstopped the Canadiens to seven championships, including the five-in-a-row dynasty.

CHAPTER 12
BREAKING HOCKEY'S COLOR BARRIER

It was January 18, 1958, and Willie O'Ree stepped onto the ice at the Montreal Forum as a member of the Boston Bruins. At first glance, it seemed like just another NHL game, but O'Ree's presence on the ice that night was history in the making. Willie O'Ree became the first Black player to play in the National Hockey League (NHL), shattering the league's color barrier. His courage and perseverance not only changed hockey but also inspired future generations of players. This is the story of Willie O'Ree, a trailblazer who fought against the odds and opened the doors for others to follow.

WILLIAM O'REE
"WILLIE"
FIRST BLACK PERSON TO PLAY IN THE NHL

Willie O'Ree was born on October 15, 1935, in Fredericton, New Brunswick, a small town in Canada. Like many Canadian kids, O'Ree fell in love with hockey at a young age. He started skating when he was three and began playing hockey shortly after. Growing up, Willie dreamed of playing in the NHL, even though he knew there were no Black players in the league. But that didn't stop him from pursuing his passion.

Despite facing racism and discrimination on and off the ice, O'Ree worked hard to prove himself as a talented player. His speed and skill stood out, and by the time he was a teenager, he was one of the best players in his hometown. However, there was another challenge that almost ended his hockey career before it even started: a severe eye injury.

At the age of 19, while playing junior hockey, O'Ree was hit in the face by a puck, which left him blind in his right eye. Doctors told him he would never be able to play hockey again, but Willie wasn't ready to give up. He kept his injury a secret, fearing it would end his career, and continued playing with only one good eye. His dream of making it to the NHL was still alive, and he wasn't going to let anything stop him.

Willie O'Ree's path to the NHL was filled with obstacles. Being Black in a predominantly white sport, O'Ree faced constant racism from fans, opponents, and even some teammates. People yelled racial slurs at him from the stands, and players tried to target him on the ice.

But instead of letting the hate get to him, O'Ree used it as motivation to prove that he belonged in the league. Another challenge O'Ree faced was overcoming his injury. Playing at the highest level with only one good eye was no easy task, especially in such a fast-paced, physical game. O'Ree had to adjust his style of play, using his speed and hockey sense to compensate for his limited vision. His resilience and determination impressed coaches and teammates alike, but breaking into the NHL was still an uphill battle.

In 1958, O'Ree got his big break. The Boston Bruins called him up from the Quebec Aces, a minor league team, to fill in for an injured player. At the time, O'Ree had no idea that he was about to make history as the first Black player in the NHL. All he wanted to do was prove that he could play at the highest level and help his team win.

When O'Ree made his debut for the Boston Bruins on January 18, 1958, against the Montreal Canadiens, he broke hockey's color barrier. It was a historic moment, though it didn't make headlines right away. O'Ree wasn't looking for attention—he just wanted to play the game he loved. He skated hard, worked as part of the team, and made an impact on the ice.

For O'Ree, the significance of the moment wasn't immediately clear. It wasn't until later that he realized what his presence on the ice meant for so many people watching. Black kids who loved hockey but never thought they could play in the NHL now had someone to look up to.

O'Ree's success showed that it didn't matter what color your skin was—what mattered was your talent, heart, and determination. Despite the excitement of making history, O'Ree's journey in the NHL wasn't easy. He only played two games in the 1957-58 season before returning to the minors. But three years later, in the 1960-61 season, O'Ree returned to the Bruins and played 43 more games, proving that he belonged in the league.

Although Willie O'Ree's NHL career was relatively short —he played in a total of 45 games—his impact on the sport was enormous. His presence in the NHL was about more than just statistics or goals. It was about breaking down barriers and changing perceptions. For the first time, a Black player was skating alongside the best in the world, showing that hockey was for everyone. O'Ree's determination to keep playing despite the challenges he faced was a testament to his strength of character. He wasn't just a pioneer for Black players—he was a pioneer for anyone who faced obstacles in their life. O'Ree went on to have a successful career in the minor leagues, playing more than 20 seasons of professional hockey before retiring in 1979.

After his playing career, O'Ree's contributions to the game continued. In 1998, he became the NHL's Diversity Ambassador, working to promote the game to kids from diverse backgrounds and encouraging inclusion in hockey.

He traveled across North America, sharing his story and inspiring young players to follow their dreams, no matter what challenges they faced.

Willie O'Ree's story is one of courage, perseverance, and breaking down barriers. He faced racism and discrimination throughout his career, but he never let it stop him from doing what he loved. His determination to play in the NHL despite the challenges showed that anything is possible if you believe in yourself and work hard.

O'Ree didn't just break hockey's color barrier—he became a symbol of hope for future generations of players. His impact goes far beyond his time on the ice. By fighting through adversity and showing what's possible, O'Ree paved the way for other players of color to follow in his footsteps and make their mark on the sport. (Mather, 2018).

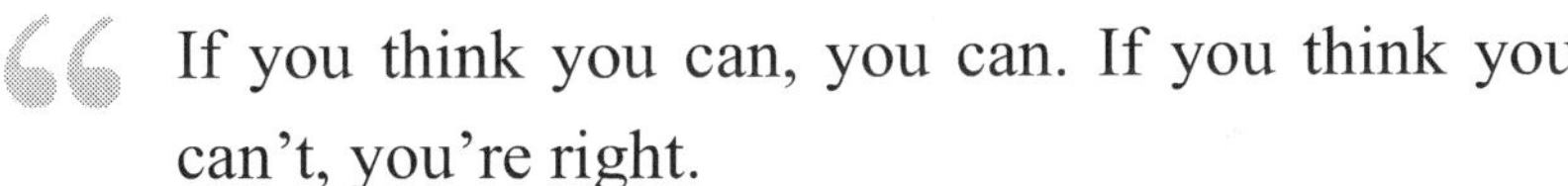

> If you think you can, you can. If you think you can't, you're right.
>
> WILLIE O'REE

CAREER HIGHLIGHTS

- **First Black Player in the NHL**: Made history on January 18, 1958, by becoming the first Black player in the NHL when he debuted with the Boston Bruins.

- **Overcoming Blindness**: Played his entire career despite being blind in one eye due to an injury, a remarkable feat in a high-speed, physically demanding sport like hockey.
- **Career in the Minor Leagues**: Played over 20 seasons in professional hockey, primarily in the minor leagues, and became a fan favorite for his skill, toughness, and resilience.
- **Long-Time Role Model and Advocate**: After retiring, O'Ree dedicated himself to breaking down racial barriers, promoting diversity in hockey, and inspiring young players from all backgrounds.
- **NHL's Diversity Ambassador**: Since 1998, served as the NHL's Diversity Ambassador, working with the "Hockey is for Everyone" initiative to promote inclusivity and provide opportunities for young players.
- **Inducted into the Hockey Hall of Fame**: Honored in 2018 in the Builders category for his contributions to the game and his role in promoting inclusivity and diversity in hockey.

CHAPTER 13
FASTEST TO 50

On a cold December night in 1981, Wayne Gretzky was just one goal away from making hockey history. It wasn't a playoff game or a championship on the line, but every fan in the building knew they were about to witness something special. The Edmonton Oilers were playing the Philadelphia Flyers, and Gretzky already had 49 goals in just 38 games. Could he really score 50 goals in fewer than 40 games, something no one had ever done? The crowd buzzed with excitement, knowing that "The Great One," was on the brink of shattering a record that seemed impossible. And then, with a flick of his wrist, the puck sailed into the net, and history was made. Gretzky had done it: 50 goals in just 39 games.

WAYNE GRETZKY
"GRETZ"
50 GOALS IN 39 GAMES

Back in the 1980s, scoring 50 goals in a season was considered an incredible achievement. The previous record for reaching 50 goals the fastest belonged to Maurice "Rocket" Richard and Mike Bossy, both of whom scored 50 goals in 50 games. That was the gold standard—no one had ever done it faster. But Wayne Gretzky wasn't like any other player.

Coming into the 1981-82 season, Wayne knew he had a chance to break records, but no one expected what was about to happen. Game after game, Gretzky seemed unstoppable. By Christmas, Wayne had already scored 41 goals in just 36 games. People started talking about whether he could break the 50-in-50 record. But this challenge wasn't just about speed and skill. Gretzky was constantly being targeted by defenders, many of whom wanted to stop "The Great One" from making history. Every team they faced knew about Gretzky's scoring streak, and they were determined to shut him down. Defensemen tried to rough him up, and goalies sharpened their focus. On top of that, Gretzky had to handle the pressure of fans and media constantly reminding him of how close he was to the record. Would he be able to stay calm and keep his focus?

Despite the pressure and the tough competition, Wayne kept going. He scored two goals against the Vancouver Canucks in Game 37, followed by six goals in the next two games. Now, with 49 goals in 38 games, Wayne stood just one goal away from smashing the record.

The whole hockey world was watching to see if he could do it. On December 30, 1981, Wayne Gretzky stepped onto the ice, knowing that history was just one shot away. The moment arrived on a chilly December night as the Edmonton Oilers faced off against the Philadelphia Flyers. Everyone in the arena knew what was at stake. With 49 goals already under his belt, Wayne was just one goal away from breaking the fastest-to-50 record. The tension in the air was thick as the puck dropped for the start of the game.

Gretzky had several chances early in the game, but each time, the Flyers' defense blocked him, and the goaltender made key saves. The pressure was mounting. Would Wayne be able to pull it off? It seemed like the Flyers were determined to keep him from breaking the record. Every time he touched the puck, defenders swarmed him. But Wayne had been in tough situations before, and he wasn't going to let this one slip away. He knew he had to stay patient.

Finally, in the third period, Gretzky saw his chance. He skated down the ice with his Oilers teammates and got himself into perfect position in front of the Flyers' net. His teammate passed him the puck, and in one smooth motion, Gretzky took the shot. The puck flew past the goalie and into the net. The crowd erupted in cheers—Gretzky had done it! He had scored his 50th goal in just 39 games, setting a new record that no one had ever thought possible.

The moment Wayne Gretzky scored his 50th goal was pure magic. The fans in the arena couldn't believe what they had just witnessed. As the puck hit the back of the net, the entire stadium erupted in a deafening roar. Wayne's teammates rushed to him, wrapping him in hugs and celebrating his incredible achievement. Gretzky himself, always humble, raised his arms in celebration, but there was a sense of calm about him, as if he knew he was destined for this moment all along.

For Gretzky, this wasn't just about breaking a record. It was about pushing the limits of what was possible in hockey. Scoring 50 goals in 39 games was a feat that no one thought could ever happen, but Wayne had done it. He didn't do it by being the fastest skater or the hardest hitter. He did it by being the smartest player on the ice, using his incredible vision and anticipation to outthink his opponents.

As the fans chanted his name, Gretzky took a moment to appreciate what he had accomplished. But even in this moment of triumph, Wayne knew that he wasn't finished. The season wasn't even halfway over, and there were plenty more goals to score and records to break.

That night, the entire hockey world was talking about Wayne Gretzky. News outlets all over Canada and the U.S. covered the story, and kids across the country looked up to him as a hero.

They wanted to be just like Wayne—to play the game with skill, passion, and a love for hockey that was clear every time he stepped onto the ice.

Wayne Gretzky's 50-in-39 achievement wasn't just about setting a new record—it was about showing what could be done through hard work, dedication, and believing in yourself. Gretzky didn't just wake up one day and become "The Great One." He spent countless hours practicing in his backyard as a kid, always trying to improve his game. He faced challenges along the way, including defenders who tried to stop him at every turn, but Wayne didn't let that hold him back. For Wayne, breaking the 50-in-50 record was a sign that anything was possible if you put your mind to it. He showed that greatness isn't just about talent—it's about perseverance and a desire to be the best. And even after breaking one of the most impressive records in hockey, Wayne didn't stop working hard. He continued to set new records and inspire hockey players around the world.

Wayne Gretzky's 50-in-39 accomplishment is a reminder that with hard work and determination, you can achieve amazing things. Even if people tell you that something is impossible, remember that Wayne didn't listen to doubters—he focused on what he knew he could do. Whether you're playing sports, doing homework, or chasing any dream, you have the power to break your own records, just like Gretzky did. All it takes is belief in yourself and a willingness to work harder than anyone else. So, the next time you face a challenge, think of "The Great One" and know that you, too, can make history.

(Baggedmilk, 2020).

CHAPTER 14
RAY BOURQUE'S STANLEY CUP VICTORY

IT WAS JUNE 9, 2001, AND RAY BOURQUE WAS MOMENTS away from living the dream he had chased for over 20 years. The Colorado Avalanche had just won Game 7 of the Stanley Cup Finals, and Bourque, at 40 years old, was finally about to lift the Stanley Cup. Bourque had spent most of his career as the cornerstone of the Boston Bruins, but despite his greatness, the Cup had always eluded him. After 22 seasons of hard work, heartbreak, and determination, this was his moment. As the Avalanche captain, Joe Sakic, handed the Stanley Cup to Bourque, the arena erupted with cheers, knowing that this victory was about more than just a championship—it was the culmination of one man's incredible journey. This is the story of how Ray Bourque, one of the greatest defensemen in NHL history, finally won the Stanley Cup.

RAY BOURQUE
"BUBBA"
THE 22 YEAR
CHAMPIONSHIP
JOURNEY

Ray Bourque was born on December 28, 1960, in Saint-Laurent, Quebec, and from a young age, he was drawn to hockey. Growing up in Canada, the Stanley Cup was every young player's dream, and Bourque was no different. As a defenseman, he quickly made a name for himself with his incredible skating, powerful shot, and elite defensive play. In 1979, Bourque was drafted 8th overall by the Boston Bruins, and he made an immediate impact, winning the Calder Trophy as the NHL's top rookie.

Bourque's career with the Bruins was nothing short of legendary. For over two decades, he was the face of the franchise, known for his leadership, skill, and dedication to the game. He won the Norris Trophy as the NHL's best defenseman five times, made countless All-Star appearances, and was a dominant force on the ice. But despite all his personal success, there was one thing missing: a Stanley Cup. The Bruins came close several times during Bourque's career, reaching the Stanley Cup Finals in 1988 and 1990, but both times they fell short, losing to the Edmonton Oilers. As the years passed, it seemed like Bourque's dream of lifting the Cup might never come true. He was one of the best players the game had ever seen, but without a championship, his career felt incomplete.

By the time the 1999-2000 season rolled around, Bourque knew he didn't have many years left to chase his dream.

In March 2000, in a move that shocked the hockey world, the Bruins traded Bourque to the Colorado Avalanche—a team with a strong chance of winning the Cup. Bourque left Boston with one goal in mind: finally winning the Stanley Cup.

The trade to Colorado was bittersweet for Bourque. After spending 21 years with the Bruins, it was difficult to leave the city where he had become a legend. But at the same time, Bourque knew that his best chance of winning the Cup was with the Avalanche. Colorado was a powerhouse team, led by stars like Joe Sakic, Peter Forsberg, and Patrick Roy. They had already won the Stanley Cup in 1996, and with Bourque's addition, they had a real shot at winning again.

Bourque's first season with the Avalanche ended in heartbreak. Despite a strong playoff run, Colorado fell short, losing in the Western Conference Finals to the Dallas Stars. Bourque was devastated. He had come so close, but the Cup still remained out of reach. After the loss, Bourque considered retiring, but his teammates convinced him to give it one more shot. He decided to return for the 2000-2001 season, determined to make one final push for the championship.

The 2000-2001 season was a special one for the Avalanche. They finished with the best record in the NHL, and Bourque played a key role in their success. He was 40 years old, but he still played like one of the best defensemen in the league. The Avalanche entered the playoffs as the favorites to win the Cup, but the road to victory was far from easy.

In the Stanley Cup Finals, Colorado faced the New Jersey Devils, the defending champions. The series was a grueling back-and-forth battle, and by the time Game 7 arrived, both teams were exhausted. For Bourque, this was it—his last chance to win the Stanley Cup. Everything he had worked for over his 22-year career came down to this one game.

Game 7 of the 2001 Stanley Cup Finals was held in Denver, and the atmosphere was electric. The Avalanche knew what was at stake, not just for the team but for Bourque. His teammates wanted to win the Cup just as much for him as they did for themselves. From the opening faceoff, the Avalanche came out flying. They played with intensity and determination, knowing they had to leave everything on the ice.

As the game progressed, Colorado took control. Alex Tanguay scored twice, and Joe Sakic added another goal, giving the Avalanche a commanding lead. But as the clock ticked down, all eyes were on Ray Bourque. He played his usual solid game on defense, making smart plays and blocking shots, but his focus was on one thing: winning the Cup. When the final buzzer sounded, the Avalanche had won 3-1, and the Stanley Cup was theirs. Bourque, overwhelmed with emotion, collapsed to the ice as his teammates rushed to celebrate. After 22 seasons, Bourque's dream had finally come true—he was a Stanley Cup champion.

The most memorable moment of the night came during the Stanley Cup presentation. Normally, the team captain is the first player to lift the Cup, but in a show of incredible respect, Joe Sakic handed the Cup directly to Ray Bourque. As Bourque lifted the Stanley Cup high above his head, the crowd erupted in cheers. It was a moment of pure joy and triumph—not just for Bourque, but for hockey fans everywhere who had watched him chase this dream for so long.

Bourque skated around the ice with the Cup, tears streaming down his face. He had finally done it. After years of coming so close, after all the heartbreak and near-misses, Bourque had achieved the one thing he had wanted most in his career. His teammates and coaches hugged him, knowing how much this victory meant. For Bourque, the moment was the perfect ending to his storied career. He had given everything to the game of hockey, and now, he was going out as a champion.

Ray Bourque's journey to winning the Stanley Cup is a testament to perseverance, hard work, and never giving up on your dreams. For 22 seasons, he was one of the best players in the NHL, but the Stanley Cup always seemed just out of reach. Instead of giving up or letting the disappointment get to him, Bourque kept pushing forward, knowing that one day his moment would come.

Bourque's story shows us that success doesn't always come easy. Sometimes, it takes years of hard work and dedication to achieve your goals. But if you keep believing in yourself and stay determined, even the biggest dreams can come true. (McIndoe, 2024)·

> It took me 22 years to win the Stanley Cup, and it was worth every minute.
>
> RAY BOURQUE

CAREER HIGHLIGHTS

- **Outstanding NHL Debut with the Boston Bruins**: Made an immediate impact in his rookie season in 1979-80, winning the Calder Trophy as the NHL's Rookie of the Year.
- **Boston Bruins Captain**: Named captain of the Bruins in 1985, a role he held for over a decade, demonstrating his leadership and dedication to the team.
- **Norris Trophy Dominance**: Won the Norris Trophy five times (1987, 1988, 1990, 1991, 1994) as the league's best defenseman, showcasing his exceptional skill and consistency.
- **Enduring Success and Longevity**: Played 21 seasons with the Bruins, becoming the franchise leader in games played, points, and assists.
- **All-Time Leader in Points by a Defenseman**: Retired as the NHL's all-time leader in points by a defenseman, with 1,579 points over his 22-season career.

- **19-Time NHL All-Star**: Selected to the NHL All-Star Game 19 times, an extraordinary accomplishment reflecting his sustained excellence.
- **Hockey Hall of Fame Induction**: Inducted into the Hockey Hall of Fame in 2004, recognized as one of the greatest defensemen in the history of the game.

CHAPTER 15
THE COMEBACK KIDS

Imagine being down 3-0 in a series, with everyone counting you out, thinking you've already lost. That was the situation the Toronto Maple Leafs faced in the 1942 Stanley Cup Finals. They were up against the Detroit Red Wings, one of the toughest teams in hockey, and they had lost the first three games of the series. Just one more loss, and their season would be over. No team had ever come back from a 3-0 deficit to win the Stanley Cup before. But the Maple Leafs weren't ready to give up. Instead, they made history with one of the greatest comebacks in sports. This is the story of how the Comeback Kids became legends.

TORONTO MAPLE LEAFS
"LEAFS"

The Toronto Maple Leafs were already one of the most famous teams in hockey by the time the 1942 Stanley Cup Finals rolled around. Coached by the legendary Hap Day, the Leafs were known for their skill and toughness. Their roster was filled with stars, including Syl Apps, a speedy forward and their captain, and Turk Broda, their unbeatable goaltender.

The Leafs had won the Stanley Cup before, but 1942 was different. World War II was happening, and some of the Leafs' best players were away serving their country. But they still had enough talent to make it all the way to the Stanley Cup Finals, where they faced the Detroit Red Wings. The Red Wings were no easy opponent. They were strong, fast, and determined, and they took control of the series from the start.

In Game 1, the Red Wings defeated the Leafs 3-2. Game 2 wasn't much better, with Detroit winning 4-2. By the time Game 3 ended, the Leafs had lost again, this time 5-2, and they were now trailing 3-0 in the series. One more loss, and their dream of winning the Stanley Cup would be over. The Leafs were in a tough spot, and everyone believed the series was as good as done.

The Leafs faced one of the toughest challenges in sports: coming back from a 3-0 deficit in the Stanley Cup Finals. No team had ever done it before, and the odds were completely against them. The Red Wings were playing with confidence, knowing they needed just one more win to lift the Cup.

On the other hand, the Maple Leafs were under immense pressure. They had no room for error—if they lost even one more game, their season would be finished.

But instead of giving up, something remarkable happened. In the locker room after Game 3, Hap Day and the team's leaders gathered the players together and had a heart-to-heart talk. They weren't going to let this series end without giving everything they had. The message was clear: every player needed to dig deep, believe in themselves, and take it one game at a time. It wasn't going to be easy, but the Leafs still believed they had a chance.

The Leafs knew that to turn the series around, they had to play perfect hockey. They needed their defense to step up, their goaltending to be unbeatable, and their forwards to score when it mattered most. But more than anything, they needed to believe in themselves. This was a test of their heart, grit, and teamwork. If they could stay focused, they might just pull off the impossible.

The turning point came in Game 4, which was played on Detroit's home ice. The Leafs knew that if they lost this game, the series would be over, and they would go home empty-handed. With their backs against the wall, the Leafs came out determined to show they were still in the fight. Toronto played their best game of the series, and after a hard-fought battle, they won 4-3 in overtime, avoiding elimination.

It was a massive relief for the team, but they still had a long way to go. Winning one game was a start, but they needed three more victories to win the Cup.

With renewed confidence, the Leafs returned to Toronto for Game 5. The home crowd gave them a huge boost, cheering loudly and believing their team could make a comeback. The Leafs fed off that energy, dominating the game from start to finish. They won 9-3, cutting Detroit's lead in the series to 3-2. Suddenly, the series didn't feel so one-sided anymore. In Game 6, the Leafs once again delivered. This time, they shut out the Red Wings 3-0, with Turk Broda making incredible saves to keep Detroit off the scoreboard. The series was now tied 3-3, and all of a sudden, it was the Red Wings who felt the pressure. What had once seemed like an easy series victory for Detroit had turned into a fight for survival.

The stage was set for Game 7 in Toronto. The Maple Leafs had made an incredible comeback, but they still needed one more win to complete the greatest comeback in NHL history. The excitement in the arena was off the charts. The Leafs' fans were louder than ever, knowing their team was just one game away from winning the Stanley Cup. From the moment the puck dropped, it was clear that both teams were giving it everything they had. Every shift was intense, every shot was crucial, and the tension on the ice was palpable. The Leafs, riding the momentum of their three straight wins, struck first.

Sweeney Schriner, one of Toronto's top players, scored two crucial goals, giving the Leafs a lead they wouldn't surrender. Despite Detroit's best efforts to tie the game, the Leafs held strong. Their defense was rock-solid, and Turk Broda made key saves when it mattered most. When the final buzzer sounded, the Leafs had won 3-1, completing the most incredible comeback in Stanley Cup history. The players threw their gloves in the air and hugged each other on the ice, celebrating a victory that no one thought was possible.

The Maple Leafs had not only come back from a 3-0 deficit to win the series, but they had also secured their third Stanley Cup in team history. It was a moment of pure joy, and the players knew they had achieved something that would be remembered forever.

The 1942 Maple Leafs taught the world one of the greatest lessons in sports: never give up. Even when the odds are stacked against you, and everything seems impossible, there's always hope if you keep fighting. The Leafs could have easily given up after losing the first three games, but they didn't. They believed in each other, trusted their abilities, and found a way to turn the series around.

The Leafs' comeback wasn't just about skill—it was about heart, teamwork, and resilience. They showed that success isn't just about talent; it's about having the determination to keep going when things get tough.

Their incredible comeback remains a symbol of perseverance and reminds us that anything is possible if you never stop believing. (Stubbs, 2024b).

You're never beaten until you admit it.

HAP DAY - TEAM COACH

CAREER HIGHLIGHTS

Syl Apps (Captain, Center)

- • **Three-Time Stanley Cup Champion**: Won three Stanley Cups with the Maple Leafs (1942, 1947, 1948).
- • **Hockey Hall of Fame Inductee**: Inducted into the Hall of Fame in 1961, honored for his skill, leadership, and character.

Turk Broda (Goaltender)

- • **Five-Time Stanley Cup Champion**: Won five Stanley Cups with the Leafs (1942, 1945, 1947, 1948, 1949).
- • **Two-Time Vezina Trophy Winner**: Recognized as the league's best goaltender in 1941 and 1948.

- • **Hockey Hall of Fame Inductee**: Inducted in 1967, celebrated as one of the greatest goalies in Maple Leafs history.

Sweeney Schriner (Left Wing)

- • **Two-Time Stanley Cup Champion**: Won two Cups with the Maple Leafs (1942, 1945).
- • **Art Ross Trophy Winner**: Led the league in scoring twice, in 1936 and 1937, showcasing his offensive skill.
- • **Hockey Hall of Fame Inductee**: Inducted in 1962, recognized for his scoring ability and contributions to the game.

Walter "Babe" Pratt (Defenseman)

- • **Hart Trophy Winner**: Awarded the Hart Trophy as the league's Most Valuable Player in 1944.
- • **Two-Time Stanley Cup Champion**: Won the Cup with the Leafs in 1942 and 1945, providing leadership and defensive stability.
- • **Hockey Hall of Fame Inductee**: Inducted in 1966, celebrated as one of the top defensemen of his era.

Nick Metz (Forward)

- • **Four-Time Stanley Cup Champion**: Won four Stanley Cups with the Maple Leafs (1942, 1945, 1947, 1948).
- • **Reliable Two-Way Forward**: Known for his defensive skill as well as his scoring, Metz was a versatile asset for the Leafs.
- • **Maple Leafs Legacy**: Remembered as a key contributor in one of the team's greatest achievements.

BONUS MATERIAL

Enjoy this small taste of the free bonuses included with our book! While we can only fit so much within the pages, there's plenty more waiting for you. To access all the fun facts, trivia, and quizzes, send an email to the address below. As soon as I receive your email, I'll send your bonus material right away!

Email: admin@terrifictale.com

FUN FACTS

- The Stanley Cup has its own bodyguards – It travels with a full-time security team to protect hockey's most prized trophy!
- A Zamboni machine was originally invented to clean vegetables – The famous ice-resurfacing machine started as a tool to wash produce before becoming an ice hockey icon.
- The Stanley Cup has been used as a cereal bowl – After winning, some players have eaten breakfast right out of the Cup!
- Wayne Gretzky's first goalie was his grandmother – When he was a kid, Gretzky used to practice shooting pucks at her while she guarded a homemade net.
- One goalie, Michel Plasse, scored a goal – In 1971, he became the first NHL goalie to ever score by shooting the puck into the opponent's net.
- The puck was once made of cow poop – Early versions of the puck were made from frozen cow manure before rubber pucks were invented.
- Goalie Gump Worsley refused to wear a mask for most of his career – Even after getting hit in the face multiple times, he preferred to play without protection!
- The Detroit Red Wings fans throw octopuses on the

ice – It's a tradition that started in 1952 to symbolize the eight wins needed to win the Stanley Cup.

- A Zamboni machine can go up to 9 miles per hour – While it looks slow on the ice, Zambonis can actually move faster than you think!
- One NHL game had a score of 16-3 – The Montreal Canadiens defeated the Quebec Bulldogs by this huge margin in 1920, one of the highest scores in NHL history.

TRIVIA

1. What is the name of the trophy awarded to the NHL champion each year?
2. Who is known as "The Great One" in hockey?
3. How many goals make up a hat trick in hockey?
4. Which team's fans throw octopuses onto the ice during the playoffs?
5. What machine is used to clean the ice during games?
6. Who was the first Black player to play in the NHL?
7. Which player scored the Stanley Cup-winning goal while diving through the air?
8. What is the nickname for a player who scores a goal, gets an assist, and gets into a fight all in one game?
9. Which NHL goalie scored a goal by accident when the puck bounced into the opponent's net?

10. What is the highest score ever recorded in an NHL game?

Answers

1. The Stanley Cup
2. Wayne Gretzky
3. Three goals
4. The Detroit Red Wings
5. Zamboni
6. Willie O'Ree
7. Bobby Orr
8. Gordie Howe Hat Trick
9. Billy Smith
10. 16 goals

QUIZZES

1. Who scored his 802nd career goal to break Gordie Howe's all-time goal record in 1994?
2. Which team went from last place to win the Stanley Cup in 2019?
3. Who scored the famous "Michigan Goal" where the puck is picked up on the stick and put into the net from behind?
4. Which team won the first-ever Stanley Cup in 1893?

5. Which goalie was the first to wear a mask regularly after being hit in the face with a puck in 1959?
6. Who scored the game-winning goal to give Canada the gold medal in the 2002 Winter Olympics?
7. Which team won the Stanley Cup in 1980 after Bob Nystrom scored an overtime goal?
8. Who scored the Stanley Cup-winning goal in overtime for the Chicago Blackhawks in 2010?
9. Which player scored the fastest hat trick in NHL history, getting three goals in just 21 seconds?
10. Which team stopped the Edmonton Oilers' playoff run in 1986 with an own-goal by Steve Smith?

Answers

1. Wayne Gretzky
2. The St. Louis Blues
3. Mike Legg
4. The Montreal Hockey Club
5. Jacques Plante
6. Joe Sakic
7. The New York Islanders
8. Patrick Kane
9. Bill Mosienko
10. The Calgary Flames

HAVE YOUR SAY

Thank you for choosing our hockey book! We hope you have enjoyed the fun facts, trivia, and stories inside. Your feedback means so much to us and helps other people find the perfect book for their young hockey fan. Leaving a review is quick and easy—just scan the QR code or follow the link, and in less than a minute, you can share your thoughts. Every review helps us continue creating books that inspire and entertain.

Thank you for supporting our book! :)

CONCLUSION

As we reach the end of *The 15 Greatest Hockey Stories for Kids*, it's time to look back on the incredible moments we've explored together. Each story in this book brought you closer to the legends of hockey—those unforgettable players, teams, and games that have shaped the sport. Hockey isn't just about goals, wins, and records; it's about courage, teamwork, and resilience. The greatest stories in hockey aren't only measured in points or trophies but in the passion and determination that drive players to push their limits and inspire others.

Through these stories, you've witnessed how much players are willing to sacrifice for the game they love. From Wayne Gretzky's record-breaking feats to the Miracle on Ice, each tale taught us that the journey to greatness isn't easy, but it's worth every effort. Every player, no matter how talented, faces setbacks and tough moments.

What makes them legends isn't just their skill, but their ability to overcome challenges, stay focused, and keep going even when things get tough. That's one of the greatest lessons hockey can teach us—that no matter what we're up against, we can find a way to push through.

Throughout the stories, we've seen how much players rely on each other. Hockey is a team sport, and the best players understand that they're stronger together. They know that no matter how skilled one player is, winning championships and creating unforgettable moments requires teamwork. Think back to the story of the 1980 U.S. Olympic team, where a group of young, determined players came together to take on the best team in the world. Their victory wasn't just about one player or one goal; it was about working as a team, trusting each other, and believing in something bigger than themselves.

In our own lives, teamwork is just as important. Whether you're working on a school project, playing a game with friends, or helping out at home, being a team player is a valuable skill. When you work well with others, you're not only helping the team succeed, but you're also building friendships and learning from one another. Hockey reminds us that every player has a role, and everyone's effort counts. It's a lesson we can carry with us both on and off the ice.

One thing that all hockey legends have in common is resilience. They've all faced moments of doubt, disappointment, and defeat, but they never gave up. When the Toronto

Maple Leafs were down three games to none in the 1942 Stanley Cup Finals, it would have been easy to give up hope. Instead, they fought back, one game at a time, and ultimately won the championship. Their story shows us that even when things seem impossible, we should keep trying and believe in ourselves.

Resilience is one of the most important qualities we can develop. Life will bring challenges and obstacles, but if we keep pushing forward, we can achieve things we never thought possible. The players in these stories faced injuries, losses, and setbacks, but they learned to bounce back, stay focused, and keep their goals in sight. They show us that failure isn't the end; it's just a part of the journey. When we're resilient, we become stronger, more confident, and ready for whatever comes next.

If there's one thing we've learned from these hockey legends, it's that dreams are worth pursuing. Many of the players in this book started as kids with big dreams. Wayne Gretzky practiced for hours every day on a small rink his dad built for him. Gordie Howe played hockey for five decades, showing us that passion and dedication can lead to a lifetime of achievement. These players didn't become legends overnight; they put in years of hard work, dedication, and practice to reach their goals.

In your own life, remember that it's okay to dream big. Whether you want to be a hockey player, an artist, a scientist, or anything else, your dreams are worth the effort. It might take time and practice, but with hard work and determination, you can achieve incredible things. Every time you work toward your goals, you're one step closer to making your dreams a reality.

One of the most inspiring parts of these hockey stories is how these players and teams left a legacy that lasts long after they've retired. Bobby Orr's flying goal, Maurice Richard's fierce determination, and Sidney Crosby's Golden Goal are moments that fans still talk about and celebrate. These players showed the world what it means to be passionate, dedicated, and fearless. Their legacies continue to inspire young players today, reminding us that we can make an impact on the world in our own way.

You don't have to be famous to leave a legacy. By being kind, working hard, and helping others, you're creating positive memories and making a difference in the lives of those around you. Whether it's helping a friend, working on a community project, or being there for someone who needs support, your actions can leave a lasting impression. Just like these hockey players, you have the power to inspire others and make the world a better place.

Even though this book has come to an end, your hockey adventure is just beginning. There are so many more stories, players, and moments to discover. Every season, new players step onto the ice, new records are set, and new memories are made. If this book has sparked your interest in hockey, keep exploring! Watch games, read about players, and maybe even try playing the game yourself. Hockey is a sport with a rich history, and there's always something new to learn and enjoy.

And remember, the qualities that make a great hockey player —teamwork, resilience, hard work, and kindness—are the same qualities that can help you succeed in whatever you choose to do. These stories show us that greatness isn't just about talent; it's about character. By learning from these legends, you're building a foundation for your own amazing journey, both on and off the ice.

Thank you for joining us on this journey through hockey's greatest moments. We hope these stories have inspired you, made you laugh, and maybe even made you feel like you were right there on the ice with these incredible players. Hockey is a game filled with passion, excitement, and heart, and we're glad you got to experience some of its most magical moments with us.

As you close this book, take the lessons of hockey with you: be a team player, stay strong through tough times, dream big, and always give your best effort. The game of hockey is much more than just a sport—it's a reminder that we're capable of amazing things when we believe in ourselves and work together.

So, here's to the next chapter in your own story. Who knows? Maybe one day, you'll be the one inspiring others with your own great achievements. Until then, keep dreaming, keep working hard, and remember that every goal, no matter how big or small, is worth the journey.

BIBLIOGRAPHY

Miracle on Ice - Roos, D., & Roos, D. (2024, February 22). *'Miracle on Ice': When the US Olympic hockey team stunned the world.* HISTORY. https://www.history.com/news/miracle-on-ice-hockey-olympic-game

The Flying Goal - Johnson, D. (2024, May 10). *Bobby Orr's Flying Goal.* The Hockey Writers. https://thehockeywriters.com/bobby-orr-flying-goal-iconic/

The Great One Hits 802 - Stubbs, D. (2024, March 22). Gretzky passed Howe for 1st on NHL goal list 30 years ago. *NHL.* https://www.nhl.com/news/wayne-gretzky-passed-gordie-howe-for-first-on-nhl-goal-list-30-years-ago

Fastest To 50 - Baggedmilk. (2020, December 30). NHL History: Wayne Gretzky hits 50 goals in 39 games. *OilersNation.* https://oilersnation.com/news/nhl-history-wayne-gretzky-hits-50-goals-in-39-games

The Golden Goal - Remembering Sidney Crosby's golden goal. (2017, February 28). *CBC.* https://www.cbc.ca/sports/olympics/winter/sidney-crosby-golden-goal-1.4002851

The 10 Point Night - Seide, J. (2024, September 10). *Darryl Sittler's magical 10-Point game.* The Hockey Writers. https://thehockeywriters.com/darryl-sittler-record-10-point-nhl-game/

The Game That Never Ended - Roche, S. (2024, May 28). *Longest NHL games in the Post-Expansion era.* The Hockey Writers. https://thehockeywriters.com/longest-hockey-games-nhl-playoffs/

BIBLIOGRAPHY

The Legendary Career of Mr. Hockey - Hub, O. C. (2024, March 26). The Legend of Gordie Howe: a hockey icon's legacy - Ozzy's Collectible Hub - Medium. *Medium*. https://medium.com/@ozzycollectiblehub/the-legend-of-gordie-howe-a-hockey-icons-legacy-da6fbca3d551

The 44-Year-Old Goalie Who Saved the Day - Anderson, D. (2019, December 19). The day the coach played goalie. *Sports Illustrated Vault | SI.com*. https://vault.si.com/vault/1961/04/03/the-day-the-coach-played-goalie

Overtime Winner on a Broken Ankle - Davidson, N. (2023, August 15). Bobby Baun, who scored OT goal on broken leg to win 1964 Stanley Cup, dead at 86. *CBC*. https://www.cbc.ca/sports/hockey/nhl/bobby-baun-death-maple-leafs-stanley-cup-nhl-1.6936604

Five Championships In-A-Row - Whitten, H. (2016, April 7). The most impressive championship streaks in all of sports - ESPN. *ESPN.com*. https://www.espn.com/sportsnation/story/_/id/15153911/the-most-impressive-championship-streaks-all-sports

Jim Kyte Makes NHL History - Cowley, R. (2021, April 27). *30 Sharks: Jim Kyte Was NHL's First Legally Deaf Player*. San Jose Hockey Now. https://sanjosehockeynow.com/30-san-jose-sharks-jim-kyte-constantine/

Breaking Hockey's Color Barrier - Mather, R. D., PhD. (2018, January 19). Willie O'Ree's chance encounter with Jackie Robinson. *Psychology Today*. https://www.psychologytoday.com/intl/blog/the-conservative-social-psychologist/201801/breaking-hockeys-color-barrier-sixty-years-ago

Ray Bourque's Stanley Cup Victory - McIndoe, S. (2024, January 19). The Contrarian: Ray Bourque's Stanley Cup win was bad and more fake arguments. *The Athletic*. https://www.nytimes.com/athletic/5209595/2024/01/19/the-contrarian-ray-bourques-stanley-cup/

The Comeback Kids - Stubbs, D. (2024b, June 23). Oilers channeling 1942 Maple Leafs in stunning comeback to tie Cup Final. *NHL*. https://www.nhl.com/news/oilers-channel-1942-maple-leafs-in-stunning-stanley-cup-final-comeback

Made in the USA
Columbia, SC
12 December 2024